As When

Tom Raworth was born in London in 1. published more than forty books and pamphlets of poetry, prose and translations. He lives with his wife, Val, in Sussex.

Miles Champion was born in Nottingham in 1968. He has published three books and several pamphlets of poetry. He lives with his wife and daughter in Brooklyn, New York.

TOM RAWORTH

As When
A Selection

EDITED WITH AN INTRODUCTION
BY MILES CHAMPION

CARCANET

First published in Great Britain in 2015 by
Carcanet Press Limited
Alliance House
Cross Street
Manchester M2 7AQ

www.carcanet.co.uk

We welcome your comments on our publications
Write to us at info@carcanet.co.uk

A CIP catalogue record for this book is available from the British Library

ISBN 978 1 78410 033 9

The publisher acknowledges financial assistance from Arts Council England

Typeset by XL Publishing Services, Exmouth

dedicated to the memories of
Pat Lansdowne, Peter Gilpin and Marilù Parolini

Contents

xi

Acknowledgements

The poems in this selection are in rough chronological order, and are taken from the following publications:

The Relation Ship (London: Goliard Press, 1966); *The Big Green Day* (London: Trigram Press, 1968); *Lion Lion* (London: Trigram Press, 1970); *Moving* (London: Cape Goliard Press; New York: Grossman Publishers, 1971); *Pleasant Butter* (Northampton, MA: Sand Project Press, 1972); *Act* (London: Trigram Press, 1973); *Back to Nature* (Bexleyheath, Kent: The Joe DiMaggio Press, 1973); *Cloister* (Northampton, MA: Sand Project Press; San Francisco: Zephyrus Image, 1975); *The Auction of Olson's Head* (San Francisco: Zephyrus Image, 1975); *Common Sense* (San Francisco: Zephyrus Image, 1976); *The Dresden Codex* (Berkeley, CA: Poltroon Press, 1976); *The Mask* (Berkeley, CA: Poltroon Press, 1976); *Logbook* (Berkeley, CA: Poltroon Press, 1977); *Sky Tails* (Cambridge: Lobby Press, 1978); *Four Door Guide* (Cambridge: Street Editions, 1979); *Nicht Wahr, Rosie?* (Berkeley, CA: Poltroon Press, 1979); *Lèvre de Poche* (Durham, NC: Bull City, 1983); *Heavy Light* (London: Actual Size Press, 1984); *Tottering State: Selected and New Poems 1963–1983* (Great Barrington, MA: The Figures, 1984); *Curtains* (Durham: Pig Press, 1986); *Lazy Left Hand* (London: Actual Size Press, 1986); *Visible Shivers* (Oakland, CA: O Books, 1987); *All Fours* (London: Microbrigade, 1991); *The Vein* (Great Barrington, MA: The Figures, 1991); *Clean & Well Lit* (New York: Roof Books, 1996); *Meadow* (Sausalito, CA: The Post-Apollo Press, 1999); *Landscaping the Future* (Bologna: Porto dei Santi, 2000); *Collected Poems* (Manchester: Carcanet Press, 2003); *Caller and Other Pieces* (Washington, DC: Edge Books, 2007); *Let Baby Fall* (Providence, RI: Critical Documents, 2008); *There Are Few People Who Put On Any Clothes (starring it)* (Cambridge: Equipage, 2009); *Windmills in Flames: Old and New Poems* (Manchester: Carcanet Press, 2010); *Got On* (Oxford: ©_© Press, 2011); and *Structure from Motion* (Washington, DC: Edge Books, 2015). 'Boomerang' and 'Doctor Mends' were published in *Vort* (1972); 'Hearing', 'Never Mind' and 'Well' were published in *The Milk Quarterly* (1974);

'Surfing the Permafrost through Methane Flares' was published as a trading card by Fact-Simile Editions (2014). 'Dark Senses' is in memoriam Barry Hall (1933–95) and 'Out of a Sudden' is in memoriam Franco Beltrametti (1937–95).

My thanks to Tom Raworth for answering my questions so patiently and generously, and to Val Raworth, and Tom, for reading what follows with such thoroughness; any errors that remain are surely mine. My thanks also to David Ball, James Cummins, Thomas Evans, Alastair Johnston, Sam Ladkin, Kit Robinson, David Southern and Geoffrey Young, and to Michael Basinski and James Maynard at The Poetry Collection of the University Libraries, University at Buffalo, The State University of New York.

MC, January 2015

If there is something of which we are dispossessed, it is those things we have made, that we believe we have made: they are things that never belong to us, not before, during, or after.
—Jacques Rivette in conversation with Serge Daney, 1990

Introduction

Tom Raworth's poetry is one of the great and pure pleasures of the contemporary literary landscape. It is writing that gets its work done quickly and cleanly, is neither didactic nor 'difficult', and stimulates the mind as much as the eye and ear. The present selection spans Raworth's writing of some fifty years, from the 'preternaturally wise'[1] lyrics of the 1960s, through the blunt, profound and frequently hilarious poetry and prose of the seventies, to the more socially and politically outward poems—fierce and tender by turns—of the eighties and nineties, and his tersely telescoped writing of the twenty-first century. From first page to last it is clear that padding out the poem has never been an option: Raworth's movement through time is towards ever greater compression—a restless homing-in on a perceived centre he has described as 'pure politics'.[2] Boundaries between poem, journal entry and notation of atmospheric buzz are thrillingly dissolved, so that poems become entirely congruent with a tracking of the poetic signal. Fragments of language are flung at the poem in a precisely controlled effort to see what might stick; these fragments are held in place by asterisks (stars) until Raworth senses longer poems beginning to build—an internal shift he has described as instinctive rather than intentional.[3]

Raworth himself has steered admirably clear of the factionalism that so often characterises the poetry world, having no use for such markers as 'us' and 'them'. That he has been hard to pin down over the years is evidenced by the various labels critics have attempted to stick on his work: 'mid-Atlantic', 'Black Mountain', 'New York', 'Surrealist', 'Minimalist', 'Language',

1   The phrase is Charles Olson's, in response to Raworth's first collection, *The Relation Ship* (London: Goliard Press, 1966).
2   'I have never reached the true centre, where art is pure politics.' 'Letters from Yaddo' (April–May 1971), *Visible Shivers* (Oakland, CA: O Books, 1987), n.p.
3   Tom Raworth to Kit Robinson, 10 August 1982. Robinson quotes and draws from this unpaginated typewritten letter in his biographical essay 'Tom Raworth', *Dictionary of Literary Biography* 40 (*Poets of Great Britain and Ireland since 1960*), ed. Vincent B. Sherry, Jr. (Detroit: Gale Research Company, 1985), pp. 459–68. The letter remains in Robinson's possession.

'Californian'.[4] Some at least of Raworth's early influences are discernible: the ease with which the stuff of the day attaches itself to the poem might be traced to Apollinaire, and he clearly found fellow travellers in the New American Poetry of the Beats, the New York School, et al. With his close friends and contemporaries David Ball, Piero Heliczer and Anselm Hollo he shares a predilection for lowercase letters and an aversion to punctuation. But as he has made clear, influence, for him, is a matter of 'thought in common' rather than 'models to copy in terms of style or form'.[5]

Raworth subscribes to no theories and propounds none of his own—'Theory leads to rules', as he has put it[6]—and has long maintained that he has no public opinions about poetry, either his own or anyone else's. Of his process he has written: 'My "method" is the essence of simplicity. I write down fragments of language passing through my mind that interest me enough after thought has played with them for me to imagine I might like to read them. What form that documentation takes doesn't interest me as an intention, but only as the most accurate impression of the journey of interest.'[7] Elsewhere he has stated: 'Sometimes I start with a title, sometimes I just write the poem, then think of a title'[8] and 'Boredom, trust and fun are the key words somehow.'[9]

Thomas Moore Raworth was born on 19 July 1938 in Bexleyheath, south-east London. His mother, Mary Raworth, née Moore, grew up in Dublin in a large Republican family that lived on the North Circular Road in a tenement building whose basement room was occupied by Sean O'Casey.[10] As a teenager

4   Raworth to Robinson, n.p.
5   Ibid., n.p.
6   'Tom Raworth', *Talking Poetry: Conversations in the Workshop with Contemporary Poets*, ed. Lee Bartlett (Albuquerque: University of New Mexico Press, 1987), p. 160.
7   Raworth to Robinson, n.p.
8   'Tom Raworth', p. 150.
9   'Tom Raworth—An Interview', interview by Barry Alpert, 11 February 1972, *Vort* 1 (Fall 1972), p. 39.
10   Raworth learned from Garry O'Connor's 1988 biography of O'Casey, *Sean O'Casey: A Life*, that the characters in *Juno and the Paycock* were based on his mother's family.

she ran messages for the rebel forces during the 1916 Easter Rising. In the mid-1930s she left for London where she met Thomas Alfred Raworth, a Londoner from Hammersmith who had left school at fourteen to work first as a museum assistant and, later, as a solicitor's clerk for Budd, Brodie and Co. at 33 Bedford Row in Holborn. Despite his lack of formal education he was highly literate and possessed of a photographic memory; in later life he deciphered Gerard Manley Hopkins's handwriting and prepared the typescript for an edition of Hopkins's *Sermons and Devotional Writings*.[11]

Raworth grew up in a semi-detached redbrick house on Avondale Road in Welling, on the border between London and North West Kent. Both parents were Roman Catholic—his father had converted—and Welling had a large Catholic population at the time: there were May Processions through the town and several Irish families living nearby.[12] When he was eighteen months old his father left to serve as a radio operator with the XIV Army in India, Burma and Ceylon, returning when Raworth was seven. He attended the local Catholic primary school, St Stephen's, most of whose teachers were Filles de Jésus.[13] The classes were small because many children had been evacuated to the countryside to escape the German bombing. Raworth made his first visit to Ireland in 1946—visiting the Easter Rising sites—and, after taking the 11-plus in 1949, was awarded a scholarship to St Joseph's Academy, a grammar school in Blackheath run by the De La Salle Brothers. St Joseph's was reached by 89 bus over Shooters Hill, with St Paul's Cathedral then the largest building for miles around. Despite some interest in physics and chemistry, Raworth found school boring. A classmate, Higgins, brought in books and magazines, and something by Dylan Thomas struck a chord, even if it was soon

11 'Tom Raworth, 1938–', *Contemporary Authors Autobiography Series*, vol. 11 (Detroit: Gale Research, 1990), p. 310.
12 Raworth grew up to consider himself more Irish than English. He took out an Irish passport in 1990.
13 One of the lay teachers, Miss Firth, would, with the help of Raworth's mother, have him reading at the age of four and a half. Rudyard Kipling's *Kim* and Richard Jefferies's *Bevis* were favourite books by the time he was eight.

damped by the teenage need to reject all forms of culture as manifested in his parents' tastes. He took up the piano and read a lot of science fiction.

Raworth left St Joseph's in 1954 during his first term as a sixth-former and got a job as a claims clerk with the Law Accident Insurance Society on the Strand. A succession of short-lived jobs followed—packing jewellery and canned goods, selling high-end china at Thomas Goode in Mayfair, labouring on a construction site—until, in late 1955, he failed the army medical for National Service when a hole was found in his heart. This was sewn up the following year at Brompton Hospital by Sir Russell Brock, one of the pioneers of open-heart surgery (Raworth was the third person in Britain to undergo the procedure and is its longest survivor). After a few weeks' convalescence he started work at Eros Films on Wardour Street, booking films into cinemas around the country. Jazz (modern British: Joe Harriott, Tubby Hayes, Phil Seamen) and clothes (Italian suits and Fred Perry) were interests, and evenings were spent going to clubs and hanging around with friends.

In 1957 Raworth took a job at the Wellcome Foundation, a pharmaceutical manufacturer on Euston Road, where he met Ken Lansdowne, a sailor recently returned from Suez. They worked alone in a small basement room, ostensibly typing lists of drugs returned. Left to his own devices for much of the day, Raworth took long walks across London and embarked on a collaborative secret-agent novel (parts of which would later appear in his prose book *A Serial Biography*) with another workmate, Nigel Black. Together they livened the largely empty workday by sending chunks of Beckettian prose through Wellcome's internal mail system (Raworth had read Beckett's 'Dante and the Lobster' and 'Echo's Bones' in the first issue of *Evergreen Review*, published that year). One day, after workmen started bricking up the basement doorway, oblivious to the typists below, Raworth and Lansdowne were retrieved and 'promoted' to the transport department.

Raworth's interest in poetry was reawakened after buying the second issue of *Evergreen Review*—the landmark 'San Francisco Scene' issue—from Tony Godwin's Better Books on Charing Cross Road. He bought the issue for Ralph J. Gleason's article on

San Francisco jazz, but also found writing by Allen Ginsberg, Jack Kerouac, Jack Spicer and Philip Whalen, among others. Around this time he looked at Dada, Surrealism and their precursors, finding Apollinaire, Jarry, Rimbaud and Schwitters of interest, and began to browse the Charing Cross bookshops more regularly. Better Books and nearby Zwemmer's were occasional sources of interesting magazines: *Botteghe Oscure*, *Migrant*, *New Departures*.

In summer 1959 Raworth met Margaret Valarie Murphy in a lift on his lunch break and they were married a few weeks later— events Raworth regards as the most fortunate of his life (Val remains the only person whose tastes and opinions he trusts). The following year they moved into two damp basement rooms on Amhurst Road in Hackney. That December Raworth read Edward Dorn's poem 'Vaquero' in *Between Worlds* (edited by Gilbert Neiman in Puerto Rico) and wrote to Dorn at the Santa Fe address given in the contributors' notes, the start of a long— sometimes daily—correspondence (some of Raworth's letters to Dorn also appear in *A Serial Biography*) and a lifelong friendship. Dorn quickly put Raworth in touch with Robert Creeley, who put him in touch with Charles Olson, LeRoi Jones and Fielding Dawson, among others. Raworth read poems by Anselm Hollo in Matthew Mead and Malcolm Rutherford's *Satis*, and wrote to him care of the editors; on 4 February 1961 they met at Jeremy Robson's first 'Poetry and Jazz' event at Hampstead Town Hall.[14]

Raworth began to think about starting his own magazine to publish writers he was interested in: Christopher Logue and Alan Sillitoe in England; Ginsberg, Gregory Corso and Frank O'Hara in the United States. He bought a 5" by 4" Adana press and taught himself how to set type and print, and, with a hundred pounds from Val's stepfather—a late wedding present— acquired a larger (11" by 8") treadle press. Raworth has suggested that the desire to print letterpress might be genetic:[15] his father had wanted to be a printer, and one of his ancestors, Ruth

14 The readers were Dannie Abse, Pete Brown, Anselm Hollo, Spike Milligan, Adrian Mitchell, Lydia Pasternak Slater, Jeremy Robson and Jon Silkin.

15 See 'Tom Raworth speaks to Andy Spragg', *Misosensitive.blogspot.com*, 21 January 2011, http://misosensitive.blogspot.com/2011/01/tom-raworth-speaks-to-andyspragg.html.

Raworth, printed Milton's first collection of poems in 1645. The first thing Raworth printed—in 1961, on the Adana, under the name Matrix Press—was two short poems by Pete Brown, the *Pete Brown Sample Pack*, in a run of six copies. This was followed by the first issue of Raworth's magazine *Outburst*, with contributions from Creeley, Dawson, Dorn, Hollo, Denise Levertov and Olson, among others, many appearing in print in Britain for the first time. Raworth set the type on the floor at 167 Amhurst Road, two pages at a time (there wasn't enough type for more), which he took to the Wellcome Foundation the next day and printed after work, on the treadle press, housed in a friend's print shop off Oxford Street.

Ginsberg and Corso stopped off in London on their way back from Tangier later that year, and Raworth, Corso and Hollo collaborated on a satirical/cut-up issue of *Outburst*, *The Minicab War*. Hollo introduced Raworth to David Ball, a New Yorker studying French literature at the Sorbonne, and Ball put him in touch with Piero Heliczer, who was letterpress-printing books in Paris as the Dead Language Press. Raworth had begun to 'write things that interested [him] to read'[16] and in early 1963 he showed one of them ('You Were Wearing Blue') to Hollo and Gael Turnbull over a drink at the Orange Tree on North Gower Street—the first time he shared his poetry with anyone outside his family. Hollo was enthusiastic.

Matrix Press published a further issue of *Outburst* and several books (by Ball, Dorn, Heliczer and Hollo) between 1961 and summer 1964, before Raworth felt that the press had run its course. He did some jobbing printing, including a catalogue for Op artist Michael Kidner, and corresponded with J.H. Prynne (who had written to congratulate him on *Outburst* in 1961). At a reading by Jonathan Williams and John Hollander at the American Embassy's USIS Library on Grosvenor Square, Williams introduced him to the painter and filmmaker Barry Hall, recently returned from a year in San Francisco where he had shown at Billy Jahrmarkt's Batman Gallery and met many of the artists and writers associated with the San Francisco Renaissance. Through Hall, Raworth met the poet and printer

16 'Tom Raworth, 1938–', p. 301.

Asa Benveniste, a New Yorker who had settled in London in the fifties and would co-found Trigram Press with Pip Benveniste in 1965.

In early 1964 Hall provided an illustration for the penultimate Matrix book, Edward Dorn's *From Gloucester Out*. A year or so later he and Raworth began printing and publishing together as Goliard Press: they acquired a larger press, a guillotine and more type, and set up shop in a cobble-floored stable off Finchley Road. The first Goliard Press publication was *Weapon Man* (fifteen copies, 1965), a broadside of a poem Raworth assembled on the spot in the composing stick to test the press. Goliard published a substantial number of books and broadsides over the next two years (including Raworth's first collection, *The Relation Ship*, at the end of 1966), and undertook jobbing printing for Trigram, Stuart and Deirdre Montgomery's Fulcrum Press (for whom they printed the first edition of Basil Bunting's *Briggflatts*), Andrew Crozier's Ferry Press and—through Jonathan Williams and Edward Lucie-Smith—Bernard Stone's Turret Books, then located on Kensington Church Walk. While the job work did something to help keep Goliard afloat, both Hall and Raworth were working full time, Hall as a process engraver near Farringdon, Raworth working nights and Sundays as a continental telephonist in the Faraday Building near St Paul's.

Raworth left Goliard Press in 1967 when it was brought under the umbrella of Jonathan Cape. Several manuscripts he had accepted for publication—Paul Blackburn's *In . On . Or About the Premises*, Olson's *Maximus Poems IV, V, VI*, Prynne's *Kitchen Poems*, John Wieners's *Nerves*—were issued as Cape Goliard titles.[17] He accepted an invitation from Donald Davie—an admirer of *The Relation Ship*—to continue his education at the University of Essex. The university had a new literature department and Davie was keen to make things interesting: Prynne selected books for the library, Dorn was invited to teach, and Andrew Crozier and Tom Clark were among the students. Raworth studied Spanish for a year, spending the spring '68 term

17 Cape Goliard's 1969 reprint of *The Relation Ship* won the Alice Hunt Bartlett Prize, then Britain's major poetry award.

at the University of Granada. David Ball sent news of *les
événements* from Paris and, after attempts to organise an on-
campus meeting in Granada were met with disapproval (Essex
was 'radical' whereas Granada had suffered years of ossification
under Franco), Raworth left in some haste, by plane from
Malaga. Back at Essex he took the first year of a BA in Latin
American literature before transferring to the master's
programme and receiving his MA (in the theory and practice of
literary translation) in 1970.[18] Trigram Press, which had already
published Raworth's second collection, *The Big Green Day*,
published *Lion Lion*, a book of poems written in Spain.

In early 1970 Raworth was invited by Kenneth Koch to read
at New York University. After reading at the Loeb Student
Center (with Dick Gallup and Aaron Vogel), he travelled by
Greyhound to Iowa City, where Hollo was teaching, then to
Ohio, to give a reading for Ray DiPalma at Bowling Green State
University.[19] Further reading tours, on the east and west coasts of
the United States and in Canada, followed in 1971 and 1972. At
his second New York reading, for the Poetry Project at St. Mark's
Church, Raworth met Ted Greenwald—the start of another long
friendship. Back at Bowling Green again in 1972, Howard
McCord and Philip F. O'Connor invited him to be a fiction
instructor for the coming academic year, and the Raworths—
now with five children—left Colchester for Ohio later that
summer. But, quickly finding themselves bored in Bowling
Green, they took what money they had and travelled by train to
Mexico City, where, after finding a house to rent, Raworth began
work on a sequence of poems, *The Mask*. Soon after, with their
money almost gone and Val badly burned from a gas explosion,
they received a telegram from Ted Berrigan: Berrigan was off to
teach at Essex for a year; did Raworth want his job at
Northeastern Illinois University? And so to Chicago, where the
Raworths felt relatively at home and where, one day, in the
middle of writing a postcard to Merrill Gilfillan, Raworth began

18 Raworth translated Vicente Huidobro's *Tres inmensas novelas* along with
    four sections of *The Penguin Book of Latin American Verse* (1971).
19 Raworth and DiPalma had corresponded after the publication of DiPalma's
    first book, *MAX* (Iowa City: Body Press, 1969).

work on a long poem, *ACE*.[20] In May 1974 Raworth travelled to Budapest for a month to work on translations with Gyula Kodolányi. He stopped off in London and stayed with Barry Hall, who read *ACE*, liked it, and offered to publish it under their old Goliard imprint.[21] Back in Chicago, Raworth was invited to a poetry festival in Austin, Texas, where he met Christopher Middleton and David Wevill, who invited him to teach there.

The Raworths spent summer 1974 with the Dorns in San Francisco at their apartment on Geary Boulevard at Masonic Avenue. Dorn introduced Raworth to the activist and master printer Holbrook Teter and the artist-engraver Michael Myers, publishers of Zephyrus Image, who lived next door. Raworth was very much involved with the press in 1974–75: Teter and Myers were brilliantly inventive printers and ideal collaborators—the rapport between Raworth and Myers was such that they could work without speech. ZI published some of Raworth's most idiosyncratic books, along with a slew of smartly irreverent and highly covetable ephemera.[22] In the autumn Raworth took up Middleton and Wevill's invitation, but for various reasons—the heat and humidity, the university, the people—Texas proved to be intolerable, and the Raworths found themselves back in San Francisco in January 1975. They stayed on Geary for a few months before moving to Holbrook and Joan Teter's cabin in Camp Meeker, Sonoma County. In early 1976 the Teters sold their cabin and the Raworths moved back to the city, where Raworth began another long poem, *Writing*. More odd jobs followed: human guinea pig for an eye hospital, stacking and mailing comics—Robert Crumb, S. Clay Wilson—for Ron Turner's Last Gasp distribution.

In spring 1977 Raworth flew to England to read at the Cambridge Poetry Festival; a few weeks later he received an invitation to be poet in residence at King's College. After five years away, the Raworths found themselves back in England. There were friends in town (John Barrell, Harriet Guest, John

20 'Tom Raworth, 1938–', p. 305.
21 All but thirty-five copies of this edition were destroyed by a flash flood the following summer; a second edition was published by The Figures in 1977.
22 See Alastair Johnston, *Zephyrus Image: A Bibliography* (Berkeley, CA: Poltroon Press, 2003).

James, Jeremy Prynne) and Raworth's duties at King's were light, although students (Geoffrey Ward, John Wilkinson) occasionally came by. Raworth finished *Writing* and began another long poem, *Catacoustics*. In early 1978 he was invited to poetry festivals in Rotterdam, where he met Harry Hoogstraten and caught up with Heliczer, and Amsterdam, where he met Franco Beltrametti, Corrado Costa, Rita degli Eposti and John Gian. An artist and architect as well as a poet, Swiss-born Beltrametti would prove to be the fourth and last person—after Hall, Myers and Teter—Raworth would find himself able to work with.

In the early eighties Raworth corresponded with Claude Royet-Journoud and Dominique Fourcade, becoming close friends with them and with Anne-Marie Albiach. He read with Beltrametti in Venice and Udine, and visited France, Italy and Switzerland regularly throughout the decade, in addition to undertaking more reading tours in Canada and the United States. In 1984 The Figures published *Tottering State: Selected and New Poems 1963–1983*, an expanded edition of which was published in Britain by Paladin in 1988.[23] Between 1986 and 1991, Raworth published 116 issues of *Infolio*, an arts magazine consisting of a single A5 card folded to A6 dimensions. The first forty issues appeared daily, making *Infolio* the world's first daily arts magazine.

In 1996 Roof Books published Raworth's *Clean & Well Lit: Selected Poems 1987–1995*. In 1999 Porto dei Santi in Bologna presented him with the first Poetry Skipper gold medal for Services to International Poetry. In 2007 he was awarded the Antonio Delfini Prize for Lifetime Achievement, and in 2014, the N.C. Kasser Lyric Prize. He has published some fifty books and pamphlets of poetry and prose as well as selected poems in Dutch, French, Italian, Spanish and Swedish translations. In 2003 Carcanet Press published his *Collected Poems*, followed by

---

23 Feeling that he had already 'selected' his poems by choosing to write them down, Raworth left the selection entirely to trusted others: Val Raworth, John Barrell, Kit Robinson and Geoffrey Young. A third edition, including the full text of *Writing* but retaining the earlier cut-off date, was published by O Books in 2000.

Windmills in Flames: Old and New Poems in 2010. He has lived from writing—from books, reading tours and occasional teaching—for almost forty years.

Alastair Johnston has suggested that Raworth's originality as a poet might be attributed to his *not* reading Olson and William Carlos Williams—not that he is unfamiliar with their work, but, rather, that he would sooner not have his own work disrupted by a close reading of the 'greats'.[24] This is not to suggest that Raworth doesn't read, but merely that, as he put it in a 1972 interview: 'I really have no sense of questing for knowledge. At all. My idea is to go the other way, you know. And to be completely empty and then see what sounds.'[25] While he has cited Hollo's early encouragement as an influence, and acknowledged that the shape and tone of some of his early poems owe much to Heliczer,[26] his 'other way' has entailed being influenced by everything and no one.

From the outset Raworth's poetry has combined a lyricism shorn of self-regard with an all but transparent receptivity to the voices. It is writing that inhabits the present as fully as art allows; indeed, the literary recognition of the fact that we live necessarily, albeit fractionally, in the past—that light has velocity—is his alone. That his work is also built to last—is literature, of an absolute quality—is not the least of his extraordinary achievements. Kerouac may have been 'the last to try to get all the way round before the bell rang for time', as Raworth suggests in a 1971 letter to Dorn,[27] but it is Raworth who takes the decisive further step, realising that 'the shortest distance between two points is to be everywhere'.[28] That scattering, Dorn points out in his back-cover note to *A Serial Biography*, is a realism.

24 Johnston, *Zephyrus Image*, p. 92.
25 'Tom Raworth—An Interview', p. 39.
26 Raworth to Robinson, n.p.
27 Raworth, 'Letters from Yaddo', n.p.
28 'Continued (Subtitles)', *Pleasant Butter* (Northampton, MA: Sand Project Press, 1972), n.p.

A Note on the Selection

In the pages that follow, the reader will notice a swift transition from Raworth's poetry of the early 1980s to that of the mid-1990s. This is occasioned in large part by my decision not to include any of the two hundred or so fourteen-line poems Raworth wrote during these years, beginning with the sequence 'Sentenced to Death' in 1986 and concluding with 'Name Unknown' in 1994. All of Raworth's extant poems in this form are collected in *XIVLiners* (Brighton: Sancho Panza, 2014) and more sympathetically presented in that volume than space considerations would allow here. Also, while I regret the omission of Raworth's book-length poems—principal among them *ACE*, *Writing* and *Catacoustics*—I was unwilling to excerpt from them. The reader is directed towards the third edition of *ACE* (Washington, DC: Edge Books, 2001) and urged to hunt down a copy of *Writing*, published in 1982 by The Figures using a wonderful earlier design by David Southern's Bull City Studios, which Southern had hoped to publish in 1978. *Catacoustics*, written between 1978 and 1981 and published by Street Editions in 1991, has become a surprisingly scarce item in Raworth's bibliography. A new edition—perhaps as originally intended, printed large-scale with a library pocket on the inside back cover for *Lèvre de Poche*—and a reprint of *Writing* are sorely needed.

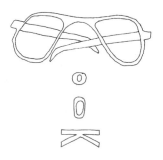

YOU WERE WEARING BLUE

the explosions are nearer this evening
the last train leaves for the south
at six   tomorrow
the announcements will be in a different language

i chew the end of a match
the tips of my finger and thumb are sticky

i will wait at the station and you
will send a note, i
will read it
          it will be raining

          our shadows in the electric light

when i was eight they taught me *real*
writing
          to join up the letters

listen you said i
preferred to look
          at the sea.   everything stops there at strange angles

only the boats spoil it
making you focus further

WEDDING DAY

noise of a ring sliding onto a finger

supposing he *did* say that?
we came by the front
sea fog twisting light above the pebbles
towards the cliffs towards the sea

i made this pact, intelligence
shall not replace intuition, sitting here
my hand cold on the typewriter
flicking the corner of the paper.   he

came from the toilet wearing
a suit, people
didn't recognise him, down the length of
corridor.   the room
was wooden, sunlight   we stood in a half circle

noise of two cine-cameras

i wonder what's wrong with her
face, she said, because
there's nothing wrong with it really   i
inhabit a place just to the left of that phrase.   from

a bath the father took champagne later
whiskey.   through the window we watched the frigate's
orange raft drifting to shore

i mean if you're taking *that*
attitude
          we rode in a train watching the dog move

noise of a bicycle freewheeling downhill

WAITING

she made it a
noise
     entering the room
as he sat holding
a cigarette   grey
smoke &
        blue
he was too   sound
of children moving so
much outside he wrote
small she
spoke he
cut a pack of tarot cards page
of (shall we go she said) pentacles re
versed meaning prodigality
dissipation liberality un
favourable news

BUT I DON' *LOVE*

but i don' *love*
you she said   there were
drops of sweat
                on the receiver
warm sun the sky
on the horizon turquoise   a faint
haze
        red trains crossed the bridge

they played war forecast music   as they
walked down the hill the brown
girls passed
                driving their own cars

the tree had not been climbed
they disturbed the dirt   it grew
like a ladder
from below the sound of water on the leaves

but she said you stroked her
hair she said she is like a
cow you are so
obvious

the gardens of the houses go down
to the stream   there are a few
allotments the path
was overgrown   they walked single file
under the north circular road   the tunnel
chalk inscriptions latest dated 1958
                                no sound
from the cars overhead

4

                                  the lake
dark red flowers   green
scum no
current a red
ball
     stationary in the middle

MORNING

she came in laughing his
shit's blue and red today those
wax crayons he ate last night   you know
he said eating the cake the
first thing nurses learn
is how to get rid of an erection say
you get one whilst they're shaving
you, they give it a knock like
this, he flicked his hand and
waved it down she
screamed, the baby stood in the doorway
carrying the cat
in the cat's mouth a bird fluttered

THREE

smell of shit when i lift him he knocks the book from my hand
i hold him up she pulls at my leg the other comes in with a book
he gives me his book picks up my book she pulls at his arm
        the other
is pulling my hair i put him down he pulls at my leg she
has taken my book from him and gives it to me i give him
        his book
give her an apple touch the other's hair and open the door

they go down the hall all carrying something

THE BLOWN AGENT

her blue gown is taking the smoke
the dust on the hem of her blue gown
blue gown—that's nice

in the low corridors of the old school   that smell
and her blue gown, poor dog
all those years the cake had lasted
we collected dust in a matchbook

immobile   the petals   the horizon   the the
lonely in the radio and no room to click my fingers
over my head   moon   moon

on a bicycle, after the car had left, her blue gown, going

AH THE POETRY OF MISS PARROT'S FEET
DEMONSTRATING THE TANGO

we were leaving on a journey by slow aeroplane
that was the weapon you had picked for our duel
flying above a gigantic playing-card (the five of spades)
from one corner to the other—our goal the gilt edge

this is a pretense (i quote your note), a cut, take the short way
because justice is what the victim of law knows is right
your stockings rasped in the silence, the engine stopped
and i wished it had been a ten of clubs with more landing space

it was a game in the air, flock wallpaper in the cockpit
outside feathers grew from metal, flapped, and we began to climb
from the mechanical smoothness to the motion of a howdah
i picked up the card, removed my goggles, and began to dance

7

HOT DAY AT THE RACES

in the bramble bush shelley slowly eats a lark's heart
we've had quite a bit of rain since you were here last
raw silk goes on soft ground (result of looking in the form book)
two foggy dell seven to two three ran
crouched, the blood drips on his knees
and horses pass

shelley knows where the rails end
did i tell you about the blinkered runners?

shelley is waiting with a crossbow for his rival, the jockey
all day he's watched the races from his bush
now, with eight and a half furlongs to go
raw silk at least four lengths back disputing third place
he takes aim

and horses pass

his rival, the jockey, soars in the air
and falls.   the lark's beak neatly pierces his eye

NORTH AFRICA BREAKDOWN

it was my desert army.   no fuss.   no incidents.
you just have to be patient with it.   take your time.
a child leaving a dirty black car (with running boards)
wearing a thick too large overcoat : grainy picture.
each night round the orange dial of the wireless.

or innocence.   oh renaissance.
a dutch island where horses pull to launch the lifeboat.
we are specifically ordered that there shall be no fast cars.
where can we go when we retire?

it was their deduction we were afraid of
so shall we try just once more?
nothing is too drastic when it comes to your son, eleanor.

and nothing works in this damn country.
no, it's not a bit like home.

YOU'VE RUINED MY EVENING/YOU'VE RUINED MY LIFE

i would be eight people and then the difficulties vanish
only as one i contain the complications
in a warm house roofed with the rib-cage of an elephant
i pass my grey mornings re-running the reels
and the images are the same but the emphasis shifts
the actors bow gently to me and i envy them
their repeated parts, their constant presence in that world

i would be eight people each inhabiting the others' dreams
walking through corridors of glass framed pages
telling each other the final lines of letters
picking fruit in one dream and storing it in another
only as one i contain the complications
and the images are the same, their constant presence in
    that world
the actors bow gently to each other and envy my grey mornings

i would be eight people with the rib-cage of an elephant
picking fruit in a warm house above actors bowing
re-running the reels of my presence in this world
the difficulties vanish and the images are the same
eight people, glass corridors, page lines repeated
inhabiting grey mornings roofed with my complications
only as one walking gently storing my dream

NOW THE PINK STRIPES

now the pink stripes, the books, the clothes you wear
in the eaves of houses i ask whose land it is

an orange the size of a melon rolling slowly across the field
where i sit at the centre in an upright coffin of five panes of
    glass

there is no air   the sun shines
and under me you've planted a quick growing cactus

COLLAPSIBLE

behind the calm famous faces knowledge of what crimes?
rain on one window showing the wind's direction

a jackdaw collecting phrases "it's a chicken!"
nothing lonelier than hearing your own pop in another country

    whose face with bandages was singing
her breath always only half an inch from the corner of my eye

LOVE POEM

there have been so many other men in my pause life
don't be frightened pause it's just my pause way
(he's going to force his *way* into her *life*—well folks
that's why we came out here to the free west

section 2

i've never said you were unattractive. that's another
distortion. i've just said unattractive to *me* at this *time*
certainly men would be attracted to you but let them have six
years of *this* sort of thing then see what they'd be like

3.

"he speaks for all of us"

4. continuing

how there are some nauseating actresses who *must* at some stage
    of their careers have played cripples (once i tried
    to let a smile be my umbrella. i got awful wet)

on to 5

like the balinese say 'we have no art, we just do everything as
    well as possible'

6. (and approaching the bend)

where is the thing i want to hold? the heroin i take is you and
    that is sentimental. which is not sex but something more
    subversive

7.

too far.　　look back.　　you've missed the point

8.　the end

yes the sun i love *came* through the window
and the last rays were *in* the park

THESE ARE NOT CATASTROPHES I WENT OUT OF MY WAY TO LOOK FOR

corners of my mouth sore
i keep licking them, drying them with the back of my hand
bitten nails but three i am growing
skin frayed round the others white flecks on them all

no post today, newspapers and the children's
comic, i sit
in the lavatory reading heros the spartan
and the iron man

flick ash in the bath trying to hit the plughole
listen to the broom outside examine
new pencil marks on the wall, a figure four

the shadows, medicines, a wicker
laundry basket lid pink with toothpaste

between my legs i read

> levi stra
> origina
> quality clo

> leaning too far forward
into the patch of sunlight

GITANES

where do all the cigarette ends go? the world should be littered
     with them
i reach for one like an oxygen mask when the trip gets bumpy
sometimes i smoke 5,000 a day, alternating between white
     and yellow
(i also drink cider and breed lettuce
here on my small farm printing fake photographs of my parents)

the ivy has grown over my inscription
lines spread from the nose, greasy, across the forehead
she's breaking up! i try to block them with cigarettes
filling the wrinkles with ash, smoothing it over, applying make-up

no, that was in '38.   i'm heading that way fast
matches all gone i vainly rub the end on my bristles
friction should do it, no, that was douglas fairbanks jnr. on t.v.

did you see him?   i almost smoked my ear
here, stepping off the pavement, damn fool, i bet he'd been
     smoking
all those books under their arms.   a rhythm of footsteps.
     sheets blowing
with cigarette burns.   and they don't flush down the toilet
     first time

well girls, *shave* those books from under your armpits
she did, and there was a small hole from which she pulled
a never ending cigarette, yellow, white, yellow, white

so we went into the labyrinth and killed the minotaur, holding on
but coming back, half-way, we found it burning
and a gnome had eaten the ash.   puff puff, puff puff

TOM TOM

awakening this morning by the baobab tree
the bright colours of my clothes fading
catarrh a slow trickle in the back of my throat

the animals whose names i know only in dialect
in this place as the day grows and the air vibrates

eyes nose and mouth the dark green of our statues
face of an ape the symbol of justice and death gone

gone chaka the welder of a thousand tribes

THE EXPLOSIVE HARPOON

régis couldn't break the pistol
corridors of panes against which the grass buckles
frozen glass sprays from his fingertips
as the blood on the leaf runs (dissolves)

cybernetic pain give me grace
the pigeon sees nothing still
caps in your mind that explode for years

wind blows in her cheeks, apparently
now is a word i like and morning, morning now
you think with my voice and all
your factories are circled by yellow machinery

your arrow's point the other
as are areas only can understand

fires in the hole behind the heather
stream overgrown with grass the daisies at an angle
the immigrant arrives   his face contained the mix to now

our town has been taken by whales, and children ride on them
and the bird on the horse through the black flames

THE UNIVERSITY OF ESSEX

for John Barrell

1. *gone to lunch back in five minutes*

night closed in on my letter of resignation
out in the square one of my threads had broken loose
the language i used was no and no
while the yellow still came through, the hammer and the drills

occasionally the metabolism alters
and lines no longer come express
waiting for you what muscles work me
which hold me down below my head?

it is a long coat and a van on the horizon
a bird that vanishes   the arabic
i learn from observation is how to break the line

(genius creates surprises : the metropolitan
police band singing 'bless this house'

as the filmed extractor fans inflate the house with steam

2. *walking my back home*

the wind
is the wind
is a no-vo-cain band

and the footstep
                    echoes

i
have conjured *pe*o*p*le

3. *ah, it all falls into place*

when it was time what he had left became a tile
bodies held shaped by the pressure of air
were clipped to his attention by their gestures

my but we do have powerful muscles
each of us equal to gravity

or sunlight that forces our shadows
into the pieces of a fully interlocking puzzle

4. *good morning he whispered*

the horrors of the horses are the crows
the bird flies past the outside the library
many heels have trapped the same way
he tolls, he lapsed with the light from so many trees

check the pattern swerves with the back
the tree that holds the metal spiral staircase swings
aloft the hand removes a book and checked it
for death by glasses or the angle food descends

5. *the broadcast*

she turns me on she turns on me
that the view from the window is a lake
and silent cars are given the noise of flies dying in the heat
of the library   the grass outside goes brown
in my head behind my glasses behind the glass in the precinct
thus, too, they whisper in museums and banks

GOING TO THE ZOO

shapes that come in the night
three tulips through my window
hair brushed in the next room

the black panther extends his leg
here is the site of the battle of maldon
mum ee mum ee mum ee

the order is all things happening now
no way down through you float in the density
so sensitively turned on the animals

HOW CAN YOU THROW IT ALL AWAY ON THIS RAGTIME?

for Jim and Nancy Dine

the sound track cut flickered to the past connection
inspiration came on to her like at coffee

the twelfth period begins with one lizard
cold blades of itzcoliuhqui

he can not move in clothes that are not his
trigger to many connections

of course the key slips through the grating
trust marginal thoughts

some like shoes will fit
the will to make out

LION LION

the happy hunters are coming back
eager to be captured, to have someone unravel the knot
but nobody can understand the writing
in the book they found in the lions' lair

LEMURES

1.
lovat on the cancered hand
lemniscus—or was it franz lehar?
i can't consult it any more

2.
it's all coming back to me, thanks
that skill again now
and in nahuatl

SOUTH AMERICA

he is trying to write down a book he wrote years ago in his head
an empty candlestick on the windowsill   each day
of his life he wakes in paris to the sound of vivaldi in summer
and finds the space programme fascinating since he still
      doesn't know
how radio works   as in the progress of art the aim is finally
to make rules the next generation can break more cleverly
      this morning
he has a letter from his father saying "i have set my face
as a flint against a washbasin in the lavatory. it seems to me
almost too absurd and sybaritic" how they still don't know
where power lies or how to effect change
he clings to a child's book called 'all my things' which says:
ball (a picture of a ball) drum (a picture of a drum) book
      (a picture of a book)

all one evening he draws on his left arm with felt-tipped pens
an intricate pattern   feels how the pain does give protection
and in the morning finds faint repetitions on the sheets,
      the inside
of his thigh, his forehead   reaching this point
he sees that he has written pain for paint   and it works better

COME BACK, COME BACK, O GLITTERING AND WHITE!

life is against the laws of nature, this we know
from nothing bangs again the heart each time
shadow and light push back across the lawn
the grass that feels them both of equal weight

and memory keeps going, clutching the straws
of similarity in taste or scent
flickering in laminates or spiralling through tracks
the perfume of you was and keeps on going

ON THE THIRD FLOOR AND A HALF

grains on a spoon
the barrage balloons
echo in the bay

a polite gesture with the tray
to let her pass
away with gentle movements

stirring into the foam
a train where they have changed
the destination plates

CLAUDETTE COLBERT BY BILLY WILDER

run, do not walk, to the nearest exit
spain, or is democracy doomed
we regret that due to circumstances beyond our control
we are unable to bring you the cambridge crew trials

if you're counting my eyebrows
i can tell you there are two
i took your letter out and read it to the rabbits

describe the sinking ship
describe the sea at night
he lived happily ever after in the café magenta

how to preserve peaches
they're counting on you for intimate
personal stuff about hitler and his gang
it's a chance i wouldn't miss for anything in the
wait in holland for
instance watching the windmills
that's more than flash gordon ever did

all those bugles blowing
in the ears of a confused liberal
so long
pretty woman
wake me up at the part where he claims milwaukee

THE MOON UPOON THE WATERS

for Gordon Brotherston

the green of days : the chimneys
alone : the green of days and the women
the whistle : the green of days : the feel of my nails
the whistle of me entering the poem through the chimneys
plural : i flow from the (each) fireplaces
the green of days : i barely reach the sill
the women's flecked nails : the definite article
i remove i and a colon from two lines above
the green of days barely reach the sill
i remove es from ices keep another i put the c here
the green of days barely reaches the sill
the beachball : dreaming 'the' dream
the dreamball we dance on the beach

gentlemen i am not doing my best
cold fingers pass over my eye (salt)
i flow under the beachball as green waves
which if it were vaves would contain
the picture (v) and the name (aves)
of knots : the beachball : the green sea
through the fireplaces spurting through the chimneys
the waves : the whales : the beachball on a seal
still : the green of days : the exit

PURELY PERSONAL

dawg put'n fleas 'n m'bed : well, evenin' draws in
red lamp : orange lamp : green lamp : cold (fill it in later)
'for the sun always shines in the country of the elephants'

all information is false
as light blows out the room after the slide performance
'n we're closer than we thought

tired and lonely here on the perimeter
tonight i couldn't give a fuck for anyone
all i see is black : you can recapture nothing

NOTES OF THE SONG/AIN'T GONNA STAY IN *THIS* TOWN LONG

the face in the dream is a name in the paper
bicycle shop smells ('sometimes my brain sings')
ice crystals bleed : these songs are songs of love

the levels write : they say
please let me in : the lights go out
(sometimes my nails sing)

ENTRY

major turnpike connections in eastern united states
audubon, witchcraft, akbar
all for san francisco

ordinary people
i have killed poetry
yes   and i had to tell you
books are dead
refer others to your own
experience perhaps
identical thoughts flicker
through each head at the same time
intelligence was the invader from space
and won   defend your planet

now that sounds intelligent

BLUE PIG

hearing the paper hearing the sound of the pen
like a seance : i will dictate these words
who dat?   she had a woollen
hat : he was so *frien*dly then

LIE STILL LIE STILL

o lady speak
for if there is a dream
then let it be
paranoia

is seeing how language works
what it means   the face of a wolf
glares back through the glass

blossom   honey
my favourite poem
is
still
is

YOU CAN'T GET OUT

this is no way
to find me
you plot your own course

in the still dark room
the blue man's skin
shows white tattoos

and you read on
and but
and so slowly

STAG SKULL MOUNTED

9.00 pm. May 1st. 1970

for Ed Dorn

mounting a stag's skull remains
the province of a tiny man
who standing on a bolt peers
across eye socket rim at antlers
(the magnetic north) that are not his
heads   east again
upon a giant brown and white
saint bernard   which leads me
to today   obsessed by thoughts
of drowning in hot water in the dark
the hound's bark drifts
through trees in the night spring air
venus is out

8.00 pm. May 5th. 1970

each evening the girl with a twisted spine
passes my window   as the weather warms
her dresses thin and shorten and useless pity
for the deformed and lonely leaves me
only this   i can not love her and her life
may be filled with warmth   i project my past
sadness on to all   the weight
of my thought of her misery may add
the grain that makes her sad   i should be dead
which is why today the roman wall
is not the stones the romans saw

11.08 am. May 7th. 1970

matthew coolly looks out from his comfortable seat in the suitcase.
it is in the case that he travels with father unwin on the missions
that require matthew to be minimised.

'found poem'

9.30 pm. May 13th. 1970

the dog is at my feet
thin paper blocks my nose, round wax bumps over me
all magical instruments must be duplicated

the way is not a direction
but a smoothing of decay

i am a ping pong ball from face to face
idea to idea   and what i do
is a disservice
                to crystallise
the doorway   the landscape beyond
to withhold knowledge   to fashion
this from the jerks of thought and vision

12.15 pm. May 19th. 1970

for Kenneth Koch

the government has explained the situation to us
pigeon in the beech tree

first a shoe shine then the whole wide world
Frank O'Hana

(the plane dropped in an effort

the government has explained the situation to us

pigeon in the beech tree
first a shoe shine then the whole wide world
Frank O'Hana

(the plane dropped in an effort

the government has explained the situation to us

pigeon in the beech tree first
a shoe shine then the whole wide world
Frank O'Hana

(the plane dropped in an effort

pigeon in the beech tree

the government has explained the situation to us
first a shoe shine then the whole wide world
Frank O'Hana

(the plane dropped in an effort

this vehicle is fitted with a hope anti jack knife device 1)2)3)4)

9.30 pm. May 24th. 1970

'and'   nobody
minds and covers blown
blossoms and leaves with love
zap zap zap zap 'and'?
the british rail insignia

'petrol burns'   'tomorrow's another day'

10.30 am. May 26th. 1970

wild elephants wouldn't drag me
in the rain gentle
men wear hats to the zoo today
i wake to read contracts
and smile that ron in his title
fused jerry lee lewis and john ashbery
with gracious goodness well
every packet bears the maker's signature
as it says on the box
of farrah's original harrogate toffee

(10.00 pm EST. June 1st. 1970
just for the record,
'great balls of fire!' was
something my mother and grand-
mother used to say (before
j. l. lewis, bless him).
                              love,
                              ron)

Noon. May 29th. 1970

i can not find my way
back to myself i go
on trying

the sparkling games
flickering at the end of my youth

12.10 am. June 1st. 1970

the time is now

12.256 am. June 1st. 1970

looking at my watch

11.42 am. June 2nd. 1970

opposites are timeless

it is the moment all time
is our selection

he had cultivated europe by the throat

9.37 am. June 3rd. 1970

this is my handwriting

1.31 pm. June 5th. 1970

for Ted Berrigan

my up
is mind made

absolutely empty

now here comes thought thought
is laughing at language language
doesn't see the joke the joke
wonders why it takes so long

but it's friday
and it's a long way down

10.26 pm. June 5th. 1970

word

10.59 pm. June 5th. 1970

10.45 am. June 6th. 1970

word: a
a: the
the: the

in
    adequate language
            i love you

8.06 pm. June 10th. 1970

poem

9.25 pm. June 10th. 1970

poem
poem

7.19 pm. June 29th. 1970

organic

7.21 pm. June 29th. 1970

education

7.22 pm. June 29th. 1970

laugh

7.40 pm. June 29th. 1970

this trick doesn't work

GREETINGS FROM YOUR LITTLE COMRADE

at the ballet he reads 'history of the ballet'
a strange convoy of desperate men and the woman they forced
      to go with them
it's true what his uncle patrick said

at the ballet her   history of the ball'
range of separate men   woman forced
it's a 'this'—cleopatra's aid

he missed the meeting
shooting along (alone)
squeezed her as

wide of the mark
at some speed
simultaneously

MOONSHINE

the plastic back
of chairs—the

of chairs—the
look at that

my moment
what it should have

storm of static
with one line clear

TAXONOMY

the albatross drawer
this is the drawer where we keep the albatrosses

THE AUCTION OF OLSON'S HEAD

a critic bought it
he thought it   was his head

37

would have explained it. But asymptosy seems destined to leave it to Vespucci. The two styles fight even for my handwriting. Their chemicals, even, produce nothing more than wax in the ears and an amazing thirst. That seems to 'even' things, for those who regard it as a *balance*, or think the wind blows *one way*. The third day of our voyage was perilous. Multitudinous seas incarnadine. But the small craft that came out to meet us contained us and went sailing into the sunset, carrying only ten pages of my logbook (106, 291, 298, 301, 345, 356, 372, 399, 444 and 453), slightly charred by the slow still silent instant. And it was in that same instant (as everything is) that we recognized that in addition to our normal crew we had a stowaway—the author of *The Incredible Max* who, alone and unaided had, on a long string, hauled the dinghy *Automatic Writing* (out from Deus ex Machinette)—or how else could he be explained? The eloquence of his moustache (you will understand) bulged neatly over & under his belt. He spoke of himself as ceaselessly sweeping up the leaves that fall from the trees. We tried to tell him about the other seasons—'Fall DOWN : Spring UP!' we made him repeat. 'Fall DOWN : Sweep UP!' he beepbada beep beep. Or the pages. Or the faces in the trees' silhouettes at night. Around us was the countryside of *Whimsy* where, huddled around leaping orange fires, the natives let their cigarettes dangle unlit in their mouths, thinking only petrol or butane could light them. Stripping bark from each native to reveal our track we followed one string of dulcimer notes after another. Nothing is lost, or confused, in this country— not the PENGUIN ENGLISH DICTIONARY, nor the RED PEN, nor the YELLOW PEN WITH GREEN INK (Patent Applied For). At night in the forest we slept, listening to the creak of our future oars. "Let us," said one of the natives whose language we could speak, but imperfectly, "build from these trees a thing which we call a 'ship'—from the wood remaining I will show you how to make 'paper'—on this 'paper' (once we set sail) I shall show you how to 'write' (with a charred twig from the same tree)—and if your grandmother is with you, here's how we suck eggs." From the shore we watched the 'ship' approach us. We set sail in small craft to meet the strangers, pausing only to write pages 106, 291, 298, 301, 345, 356, 372, 399, 444 & 453 of the logbook, charring a fair day. Afraid I think only in words : that is to say I am able to say "that is one of the things we have no word for." And when our journey takes us into the dark (en una NOche osCUra . . . roll up . . . roll up!) I am quite able, by touch, to say to myself "this is another of the things we have no word for that I've never felt before." And so, pausing nly to drop an 'o', flick cigarette ash into the waste paper basket—ash which lands in the exact top right hand corner of the only piece of paper in the basket, which I now have beside me, reading on the reverse (hidden in the basket, but the grey pattern of type through paper attracted my eyes) 'THE CHANGING CRICKET BAT—a clever sleight of hand trick which will mystify your audience.'—and look through the window at a man in a white suit turning the corner, I reach the end of my sentence. At the same moment the record changes. I type in time to the snare drum 'every branch blows a different way.' Ash fills my fingerprints making a soft cushing sound as I type on, pausing only this time to watch my fingers move, have a pain in my stomach, pay close attention to three words in the lyric. Now it is almost time for

or, indeed, as an out-of-space static. I am
writing, perhaps, the story of Atlantis : and if
you can only see the peaks, and think a detailed
description of *them* is sufficient, then grow gills,
swim down, and get over that molecular
distinction of 'the surface' and think a detailed
description of an out-of-space static ; or,
indeed, *as* an out-of-space static. I am and think
a detailed description of *them* is sufficient. The
pen scratches on the paper, the rain taps on the
window. The ship has sailed, and from inside
the beer bottle we read the label in reverse
through the brown glass : 'ƧИAMUЯT'. And
the twig from the tree outside is stationary
and dry, stuck into the neck of the same bottle.
And the bottle stands on the table (the wood of
which came from Finland) next to the
empty cigar box ('Elaborados a mano' in
Cuba) near the Olympia typewriter (from
West Germany). Until finally writing becomes
the only thing that is not a petroleum by-
product, or a neat capsule available without
prescription. And think a detailed description
of *them* is sufficient. I am writing, perhaps, the
story of Atlantis, and if you can only see, then
grow gills, swim down and get over that
molecular distinction of 'the surface'. Until

the ticket on which we saw, turning it over, the words **MAFIA MONEY** in Cooper Black type. Which meant that at that moment (the ship comes in, the craft go out—and beneath them all is Atlantis, the form of our voyage) we were thinking about Germany, and how to get there. Two scouts had been despatched to the new *Casa della Pizza* on the corner of Head Street to bring back provisions, and I was again left with the logbook. Today's happenings bear no relation to the beauty of, for instance, a brass chronometer or a sextant. But a burst of happiness comes (at the same instant as the t.v. blurts 'Cliff Richard in Scandinavia') on turning over in my papers a letter which arrived this morning from our point scout Joe. 'You're goina FIND me/out in the CUNtry' sings Cliff. The audience laughs. Do you remember the author of *The Incredible Max*? He is here too, on the telephone. But residual beams flicker 'TEEN TITANS', and the beautiful codex: "So you girls want to do your thing in my shop? Well, let's play it by ear and see what kind of 'vibes' occur." Against which can only be set the thought of the New Band of Gypsys: Jimi Hendrix, Janis Joplin, Colonel Nasser, Erich Maria Remarque and John Dos Passos. Or how do YOU think? A play with unlimited cast, each saying one line only. Or the poem that frequent deaths do not affect the bedding. Swimming around in the glass with the scent of juniper entering our lungs we screamed out. But our cries were drowned by voice-carrying laser beams which, activated by the CO_2 in our breath, boomed THE RIVER MEDWAY HAS OVERFLOWN ITS BANKS NEAR TONBRIDGE . . . THIS WOULD IMPLY THAT THE INFINITIVE WAS *OVERFLY*. *TO OVERFLOW* HAS THE PAST PARTICIPLE *OVERFLOWED*, NOT *OVERFLOWN*. The information was just in time—although in the bulb-shaped glass the pressure of the voice had forced us under the surface—for the giant finger that dipped in, stirred us around, and re-ascended to stroke the rim of the glass, created, as it gathered speed, a perfect C sharp, which shattered our prison and caused the clear sea to overfly. How neatly all the solutions are labelled 'Paradox'! And how much we owe to Adam who never bit the apple, but rolled it along the ground, thought 'wheel', and so bought us death, clothes, and 200 different kinds of washing powder. These last few nights I wake, unable to change the film running through the two projectors behind my eyes. Of course the stars were nearer before we could fly—why else should the universe expand? And what goes on behind my head, these nights when blood spatters & snails down the shiny celluloid? Mirrors lie. This voyage can only caps. I have been from one to another of my friends and I feel uneasy. I understand now that I have been dead ever since I can remember, and that in my wife I met another corpse. This is the way salt is made. We, the salt, get put on and in things. But we are our different taste. I am in Maine. Did your salt taste different today? What did you expect this to be? I am sodium—I realise now my fear and love of water. Chlorine. We have combined to save you from our separate dangers and become the sea. Sodium rode in the bus taking care not to sweat. In front of him the strange tracery ASHTRAY. To his left SAFETY EXIT—LIFT BAR—PULL RED CORD BELOW—PUSH WINDOW OPEN. He copied this tracery as the bus sped along the dotted line. Across a pale green metal bridge. To the left grassy hillocks, then pines. In the distance a black horse cropping. He counted four blue cars, one after another. The green tinted windows of the bus announced a storm. TS 536, another blue car, overtook the bus. This is MAINE, he told himself. And the selectors threw up 'an island off the rocky coast of Maine'. An exit road curved down. A truck called HEMINGWAY passed. What strange mutations will come from the grassy strip between the lanes—never walked on, fed by fumes, cans, paper, tobacco &

subtlety is only what you see looking around inside your head with a torch : beating your radar pulse there to yourself and back and describing the journey. No, that was something else. Red. Until the day I (   )ed that intelligence & intuition were the same, & passed through *that* fence. The word I choose so precisely becomes next day the key word in an advertising campaign to sell a brand of stockings, because the *word* means *what comes to mind first*. And as a 'writer' and 'artist' I should have sensed the direction of that word. As the renaissance painter should have sensed his picture on the packet around those same stockings with SIZE NINE printed across the detail which took him three days to paint. Because the stockings are always been there, and we are all USEFUL . . . & the packet was one of the things for which he painted the picture. Like the con of ecology, which has been fed & fattened to keep your mind *off*. Buy CLEAN MACHINES. So long as we are all satisfied that matter cannot be destroyed it is a closed world. 'Art' says only "This is how I do this"—and a form can be used once only. "He planted that word twenty years ago so that its weight is now exactly right"—that's the message of 'culture', the real, cold, science. The last message to come through on the old transmitter was ELECTRICITY WILL STOP . . . and we have no way of knowing if the last word was message or punctuation. So before can work the transmitter we've forgotten the message. The card retrieved from the bottle floating by said only

o

how you grow

and as we stared a foresight appeared above the o, and it became the muzzle of the rifle whose butt, as the picture tilted, was cracking Rosa Luxemburg's skull. And the circle of paper from within the o fitted first neatly into the hole of an old early morning return bus ticket, took off, was lost for an instant in a swirl of confetti, & finally settled in George Kimball's empty eye socket as he searched in the sawdust under the table for his glass eye. And the sawdust, the table leg, the confetti, the bus ticket, the rifle butt, came from the SAME TREE, whose final total of seasonal rings, said aloud, is the name of god. On the coast of Maine the stones are a foot in diameter. On the northern coast of France they are an inch. Their travels tilt the earth's axis towards another Ice Age WHICH WILL KILL THE VEGETABLES. For this is the battle : between the vegetables and the rocks. And we are the disputed territory—we, and the water we come from and are. And fire is the flint destroying the tree (though it be coal—the vegetable in disguise). And mushroom & hemp are the settlers moving west.

I'm not going to make it to the lift in time, nor change my name, and the dialogue echoes off the walls of the set. It's the front room, and the queen's picture flickers into a limp book called Jimi Hendrix because all books are dead & we live where the edges overlap. The material is transparent, but the seam is already ripping down from Orion. And I am busily sweeping up the last few words in a country without an ear, whose artists are busy filling in the colours they've been allocated in the giant painting-by-numbers picture of themselves, because they think an interview with the man (now a physicist in Moscow) who was the boy on the Odessa Steps *makes a connection*. Full moon. High tide. Because it's all gesture, and nobody ever talked in words

CONTINUED (SUBTITLES)

everywhere i go at night i spoil
a perfect wash of moon light on the ground
with lousy lines like this

the shortest distance between two points is to be everywhere

what the poet is trying to do is trace the word back to the power
—like going the opposite way to the whispered phrase in a party
game

perhaps we are a cartoon, an imitation
a flame effect electric fire

there are no allegories—there is only the event, a projection of
subjective views

☆

NO   BODY   EVERY   BODY

☆

see the
subtleties

for once
forward

the possibilities of the plots
right away

drugs is all could

☆

POEM

thicken
volition
cushion

☆

ANTICIPATION   CAN   BE   HAPPY

☆

a t.v. serial with each episode (without seeing previous ones)
directed by a different film director—but the whole thing . . .
clothes . . . sets . . . new cast

☆

PLEASANT BUTTER

i've used it
now there's no way out

DREAMING

the background doesn't matter
if the people are true

POEM

half
a
thought

SONG

if it spreads
   it's wrong
   it's only
what you do

once it spreads

voice recognised on soundtrack behind set

they don't recognise
art as it happens
in as *well*

in the way that advertising (repetition) *uses up* language sequences, so the academies want to use up *form* : the danger lies in later academies forcing others into your *form* (the content is always the same : words = true form)

random gives
faster flicker
to draw from

culture is reassurance : art is nervousness

FRIDAY

art is knowing what's *right*, not what is possible

A MODERN LANDSCAPE

when self is love
(a bird walks in the garden
across a rag smelling of paraffin

i am waiting for another phrase
to give it its
full value

eat
eat
eat
eat
eat

CHART

spike of pain
ice of mysteries
lose control

FRIEND AND NEIGHBOURS

all
different
loves

silence
is   the
motor
running

outside
it   is
again
noisy

opposites
hold   us
in   our
dimension

BIRTHS OF IMAGES AND DEATHS

for Stan and Jane Brakhage

he turns
it is the leather skullcap
on his head

i am lost
they turn through all connections
of light

in rhythm
now they walk behind the smoke
and turn

they are acting
it appears
the pit depends on her hair's weight

gold into feathers
the smoke is them
the eyes of doors open

it is clay
the city on a table
the smoke thinks

now she is perfectly lit
stone is a hummingbird
poised feeding at the image

and there is more
always on the way
a simple change like hair's death

lips under a nose
under eyes teeth
behind lips and all in the spectrum of grey

where is the lost colour?
wandering in the machine
strange boils, scurvy, on the machines

but chosen
the last chord
you must leave now

IN THE BEGINNING WAS THE WORD, AND THE WORD WAS WITH GOD, AND THE WORD WAS GOD

form of the word
is heated
and dropped on mind

the shape it burns
depends upon
memory and imagination

a perfect mix
of their solutions
is totally inflammable

so all is revealed
or we are
branded

ART IS THE FINAL CORRECTION

(hints for poets)

> : speed it up till it's faster than you
> or be the other

his terrible swift's word

GET LOST

comparisons start from mistakes
life is getting stronger until you take what
art springs from differences   you want
                         in feeling
help me   i'm a policeman

ANNOUNCEMENT

you pay for my disintegration
because i dazzle you
when every facet is completed
i can sleep inside as you bask in your own light

RATHER A FEW MISTAKES THAN FUCKING BOREDOM

giant cameras whirring
on the lens hood of each
stands a rifleman

his warning shot
as the image approaches
sounds in the past

today we are scraping
every particle from the tin
cocoa-tin telephones

smell of steam trains
unable to act his deformity
sounds every where

empty affects all thinking
whistling sounds
as the familiar voice sells its pretension

(oh guide my hand
to make these tracks
i do not understand

soft needle mind
now fills all grooves
to amplify time's wind)

DROP IN EXISTENCE

i am lonely for my replaced cells
1945, 1952, 1959, 1966, 1973, 1980, 1987

learn your language
no direction *is* home

JUST OUT OF THE PICTURE

truth must lie
in the things we tell to children

once i was my father
and my mother and so on

imprecision

but the shape
of their green hills
is determined by the waste of our excavations

HOW TO PATRONISE A POEM

begin
welcome in

appear
poem
in these lines

i will
not draw
your picture

no. the spark comes. we work together. oh it is form, form, the making of distinctions. form, the shape revealed by the detection, in all dimensions, of the boundaries of content

stunting their *own growth* . . . making *themselves* ornamental japanese trees, safe, instead of being the trees *struck by lightning*

"extra yields
extra profits"

as if what they handle
were not alive

life was the invader, perhaps, and all things that *live* were *members* of the *crew* (animals went in two by two, yin and yang) who survived through a warp into no-space between

i sense the end
down a tube
a spurt now and then

eighteenth to eighteenth
a choice
of the net's size and gauge

the ship is changing course
i have played out the games
and the old faces bore me

season to season
names flashing
i'll hammer it

so damn thin
i can see out

our enquiry
points a way
off the wheel

eleven segments
are left to trust
and imagination

lose
your   self

your   self
     becomes
your   art

then what is left

     lives

no matter how you muddy it

it clears
       and there you are

again

do you see me?
i am leaving a space
where i was   is as bad

i shall forge the blade
of my *own* substance

and it may not be a blade

i have tasted fire
goodbye, pleasant butter

TRACKING (notes)

light (drugs as only altering positions of piles of chemicals). light as feeling? i.e. pulse waves (what happens to things moving away faster than the speed of light? does light die out?). jesus, shakespeare, hitler, etc. (political waves?) going out from planet like heart beats.

light. dream being the mixed waves of feeling from other 'mind' sources during darkness—our consciousness (un is not sub) due to nearness of *clear light source* (reflected light or what? mirrors?). day—night: artificial light destroys balance (midnight sun?).

every question you ask presupposes
an alternative universe

fibonacci numbers?
1: 1: 2: 3: 5: 8: 13: 21: 34: 55: 89 etc.

saddle of *hare*?

god is the space between thoughts, no, that's simplistic. sometimes you can't understand the words but you know the medicine is right.

for god's
sake
stay open
to your time

what's done
is

☆

train

    the night

        rain

☆

nothing

lasts

☆

within everyone is an antenna sensitive to the messages of his time: art is beamed to these antennae. education should tune them: instead they are smothered with phony 'learning'. the past has no messages (yes it has—whispering smith's harmonica and a dog howling in the night).

☆

we

    are

      now

☆

not rejecting *knowledge* but what (as in research) passes for knowledge and is but an illusion. the words (knowledge, intelligent etc.) must be redefined, or new words coined.

that is sure

    clear

the connections (or connectives) no longer work—so how to build the long poem everyone is straining for? (the synopsis is enough for a quick mind now (result of film?)—you can't pad out the book) (a feature film with multiple branches: you'd never know which version you were going to see).

things of your time are influenced by the past. the artist can only go on from there and use the situation *as it is*: anything else is distortion.

i stick with de kooning saying 'i influence the past'—and it is not important for the work of a time to be available in the mass media of *its* time: think of dickens on film, dostoevsky on radio.

the true direction is always a glancing off—there must be an out—all truth is not *contained* in the language: it *builds* the language.

ahab: bringing back the *light* (whale oil?). darkness?

who's done any work on moving of food from where it grows? (connection to *land*).

plane explosion—where do the sandwiches and suitcases land?
killed by a flying gold tooth—is it treasure trove?

white connected to *light*? (link with white races fading?) the
concentrated flashes of light from blacks' teeth/eyes?

acid
or drink sweet drink
bananas and dates
disconnect battery

writing and i have a child
indigestion: fritz and su-su
        the intestine

sun leaves the leaves
send this and strawberry
chewing gum to aram

mara ot *mug* gniwehc
yrrebwarts *dna* siht dnes
sevael eht sevael nus

enitsetni eht
us-us dna ztirf: noitsegidni
dlihc a evah i *dna* gnitirw

yrettab tcennocsid
setad *dna* sananab
knird teews knird ro
dica

into the side of the waterfall
      the depth of the image

follow life
do not   despair
(the legendary cock-of-the-rock
stay *on* the wheel
do not accept the illusions
i   sol   at   ion
of conservation and ecology
(or that's the way the llama breaks)

the shadow and the sun vibrate
the circle and the shell

penumbra

dig////it

the disguises
fit tight and are sealed

testing to find what? spurt spurt
the positions of chemicals are altered

the decision
is not provoked by flicker

so why does it articulate?

what does the word truly mean?
how do we ask the question?

beneath the tight bodice
a nipple lights
the investigation closes a door

all week i've (week?) felt
the speed of writing
explanation rejects my advance

models of the past

agree to the movement
who are you?
your self faces you

any   erg
anergy

his neck was like pigskin
with the bristles still in

laurent odour

the curtains are closed
in the theatre
genetic reels
are stored in no time
and no space

but there is print through

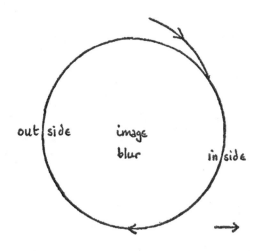

FACES CHANGE AND CHANGES FACE US
(a diary for Lewis Warsh)

the truth of your time is like a box of random lights . . . bulbs flicker on now under painting, now under music, now under journalism, now under comics, now under clothes: trying to catch it is like trying to pick up a cherry-pit with one finger . . . but at least you must try to touch it . . . *that* is the sound of one hand clapping.

ben stung by wasp. aram stung by wasp. ben and lisa teeth filled.

there are times i am lost in language, its echoes in my head, so that 'reality' becomes a curved wall around me, echoing back noise i can't pay attention to (i.e. the *direction* surrounds me).

for four or five years i couldn't read unless sitting at the piano with the book on the music rest, playing random notes.

"he can throw the gas where he thinks it will be most beneficial" (belfast)

val: "seems to me fame tends to be a lot of shits thinking you're all right."

inside this fence the power cannot reach me. i shall lie against the warm wood facing away from the source until the music stops. below the melody is the steady clop of a horse.

there are only my equals

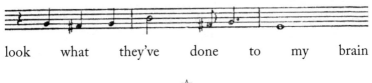

look   what   they've   done   to   my   brain

☆

paper money
in chinese
flying money

☆

perform
poor   form

☆

any thing is space   divided differently
we are   hardening of images

giving

temper

TRUE CONFESSIONS (notes)

the past is distorted rumours of the present (decay works back-
wards?)

old light coming in from dead stars
must cut down to a level
where 'i' can reflect some thing beautiful

the sea otter uses a tool (stone) to open clams
"only a sea otter really *needs* a sea otter skin"

those fairytale kings knew *exactly* what it was about when they
offered their kingdom to anyone who could make them laugh.

the critics almost invariably concentrate on what should be
subliminal—they spread the jam so thin it loses its taste—using
the past to hold you in their present.

"un deux trois—that's three in french"
with all that magnification we haven't changed the eye

look at the t.v.
that silver image you have in your home

"bawdy tec paperbacks"

comparing the arts with the roman circus (while i think of it, this isn't accurate at all—the majority of the audience doesn't want the acts changed) we are now in the period of throwing christians to the lions. jaded palates: or why 'boredom' is the key word of the era (but the ruins of the colosseum will be interesting).

assuming the past to be distorted memories (rather than rumours) of the present (any present) then *déjà vu* is a true memory fitting exactly over its event on all subjective levels, and thus a tube, or the beginning of one, through *time*.

IMPERFECT REFERENCES : AREA

the walls of the ego are the walls of the set

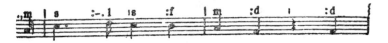

the more we are together, the merrier we shall be

IMPERFECT REFERENCES : BOREDOM

the light we see is light slowed down by thought
an instruction is always change some thing

RIOTERS   STONED   FIRE   MEN

definitions: R = a P having a pee.

☆

"'s.s. EXACT' the surveying ship" (T.V.)

☆

language swirls around us
trunk calls

☆

this is the image for that

☆

sometimes i think in images
sometimes in prose
although i don't
the academy knows

☆

PERFECTLY INTEGRATED

weld interest
to thing
do do do
into the true

☆

there are 400 cedars left in the lebanon—one of them is 6,000
years 'old'

☆

TIME ERRORS

that doesn't matter
time   gun

i confess: i have become an explainer
i have fallen onto description's
other side

SONGS OF THE DEPRESSION

there's a shop on the road
we whiz by
slowing down from our speed
a turn off's an angle

talking the song through a kazoo
the giver of which
heads for switzerland
this thought holds it together

why four lines and a stapler?
why an address book?
a bottle of brandy? why
a key ring? an ashtray?

will you sit in the sun
or write a letter urgently?
how long will the candle melt
while i listen to the band?

grab it all and don't slow down
never leave the road for what's
in a shop or a store
the road's enough

why exclamation mark four
lines and a stapler glue
kleenex an envelope
shards of god

this is my table today
this is the sound
this is the noise through
my eye that spins around

GASLIGHT

a line of faces borders the strangler's work
heavy european women
mist blows over dusty tropical plants
lit from beneath the leaves by a spotlight
mist in my mind a riffled deck

of cards or eccentrics
was i
a waterton animal my head
is not my own

poetry is neither swan nor owl
but worker, miner
digging each generation deeper
through the shit of its eaters
to the root—then up to the giant tomato

someone else's song is always behind us
as we wake from a dream trying to remember
step onto a thumbtack

two worlds: we write the skin
the surface tension that holds
                              you
                              in
what we write is ever   the past

curtain pulled back
a portrait behind it
is a room suddenly lit

looking out through the eyes
at a t.v. programme
of a monk sealed into a coffin

we close their eyes and ours
and still here the tune

moves on

LOVE AND PIECES

met language static
on the street
thinks he's one
of a new elite

you have to learn
you can not teach

"there goes the town of spanish boot"
"only the buildings"

julius reuter
service de pigeons

i can not prove a second ago
to my own satisfaction

WANDERING

terror of people leads into 'the people'
keep the message to your self
it's your journey

not to say the picture's wrong
but the hands
of the clock haven't moved

this has an archaic air like 'ere and o'er
make it fast
features formed by time's wind

dance inside the cloth
in a dull room
thin honey haze

this heavy haze
open the door
let it fight noise

lavender upon lime green
orange on dark brown
lost and am fishing

BOUNCE

the poor are painted out
the rich, powerful, and famous have their say

tomorrow will be everywhere
so why not call it today?

"hello tomorrow, this is
a wanderer among the voices"

some are pictorial
and even educational

try all the different bits

      fragmented

      sparkling

puff! i've put it out with my *hand*
and you all understand

PATCH PATCH PATCH

some evenings i think
of honour, glory, and bells

the last challenge is unanswered

cold night by the docks
captain bulb salutes another bottle

don't worry about that

in one part of the ship a phone rings
a message from another part of the ship

doppler effect

i don't know
where i can go
and sing the national anthem

everyone arrives at the ship on time
the girl, the golden-hearted drunk

"fuck it, finger, this poem *leaks*!"

FUTURE MODELS MAY HAVE INFRA-RED SENSORS

take a taxi and go fishing
how do you like that?
visit canada
hey look, i see a big moose

cat's nose is twitching
why don't you ever go
to work and earn money?
invest your money here

why don't you try it yourself?
i'm on guard duty
with the armoured car
could you give me a lift?

then we could buy some lunch
gentlemen, here comes lunch
there is all the food we want
just give me a microsecond

maybe you likee something
to eat while you wait?
of course, of course, well, well
i'll prove it to you

you sir. who, me sir?
well sir, what is the verdict?
believe me
i've never seen my sheet

tell me again, i don't get it
sorry, hotee dogs all gone
a natural using wild game
one share of wildcat oil

don't cut *me*. i never
heard of wildcat oil
broken glass, drawn stars
fine, fine, you killed him

hold it officer, it's my duty
right behind the car sir
before anyone sees me
my pleasure, you know what they say

money talks. i just don't understand
xylophone trills
another day like yesterday
we'll be in gravy

pardon me gentlemen
is there a bank
in the neighbourhood?
you drove up from hillcrest?

MIRROR MIRROR ON THE WHEEL

what is my frame?
dry hot handkerchief
pressed to my eyes

unreal
i am examining
my love for this child

who looks so like me
i am inside
his movements

now he drops my keys
and stares
at the tape deck

"all your sea-sick sailors
they are rowing home"
we hear

time, i love you
you are the way
i see the same anew

BELT

for Darrell Gray

going all the way
and adjusting
going all the way

CHICAGO

pistol whipcracks i wondered about
are ted typing below

           white snow

UNIVERSITY DAYS

this poem has been removed for further study

UNCERTAIN STEPS

not a duty, nor a purpose
nor a mis-reading of the black bird's swoop
many years in this same place

twisting a used flashcube under the lamp
for white light to eat gold
no grace in that steady clapping

to the music, to the four winds
i have waited always with birds' black
shadows keeping light from certain cells

a hand draws me into the air
among whose atoms children dance
as though they did not understand

the secret, which is what
holds everything up
into the light

FROM TIME TO TIME IN THE PAST

tree lets me hear the wind
over there where it is
i won't believe this is all there is
(the interest on eternity)

'it is' squeaks my voice

MIXED

whee! the tip of a lock
of her hair blows round
and round on the urban set
mocked up like your 'jungle'

but from deep in the tape
of tropical sounds
a good engineer brings out
first a splash in the surf

then 'we are lost' in her
father's voice: but ludwig's
ears were deadened
by the last of a species of bright birds

EVERYTHING 'UNDER' THE SUN

a likely button of yes
immobilised

all 'over' the world
some radios are off and some are on

eat what you want
learn your own lessons

if you want
don't let the revolution hold you back

NO PEACE/BLACK HOLES/EARTH CRACKS

there's a lot of things you can do
without using words—i was doing i
very hungry. the red elastic mark

LAID WASTE BY THE LUFTWAFFE

punctuated by birdbaths
facts, give me some facts
i'm down to my last
plants were grown organically
without space or fertilizer
re-creates his best-loved mimes
in omnibus. spring. leaves
spiralling through butterflies

THE ETHICAL ARTIST

kept a source book
but picked each plum

INFINITE VARIETY STALES

the narrative line is only as boring
as what's hung on it
one auk a verb met a noun
who will care for the child
so it must burn
unless called away
dissolve bridges radio squawks in the jeep

costumes are codes
in bright flexible corridors
"radio . . . your dead archer standing by"
this pigeon has flown the coop
to an image lag rapid letter breaks
orange california poppies
established his delusion

NEW YEAR

for Michael Myers

how painfully i feel both dark and light
as if my bones were boils
my outer layer quite quite dead
i see most art as slow ideas
carrying passengers i like or notzzzzzzzzzzzzzzz

"one lincoln under god etc."

the impressionist

CAP

pattern outside my head
speak to me
signaller of the word-commune

i was not aware
one lonely word outside
could call itself 'snap'

INTO THE WILD BLUE YONDER

prisoners
christmas

our
ower

pour
power

"43" he said, referring to the numbers they'd
given the background noise tapes

BOOMERANG

hands up!
what are your interests?

DOCTOR MENDS

the signs are there
for all to see
this is just
the beginning

NOT A STEP DO I STIR UNTIL THAT CAT'S BACK TO ITS COLOUR

civilization was pushing around ageing molecules saying
"lovely . . . a new patch of lung" and "aching doesn't thank"
when a sunbeam hit my son, throwing his tiny full colour
     reflection
onto the centre of the flickering black and white screen

A BLUE VACUUM CLEANER

in the scent of burning vegetables
a scratch on my nose adjusts vertical hold
while with my left eye i see long distances
to where time turns light cold

small star, someone named you
what are you doing to me?

THE BECKONING HARPOON

my muse is bored with the company i keep. i wait for her to
flash the mirrored paper in my eyes and she does this.

OUT TAKES

a tiny fifth genius

stand up
all of you
using binoculars

somebody's got to be seen around here

look
i've trapped these molecules
into my shape is

steam iron

one pound extra to use the lift

model

i know a shadow doesn't bend that way in space
      a shadow   in space

inner mist

tuesday in poetry town: some of the pages are upside down

la

speak
mozambique
trick or treak

mark

well folks, here we are on the surface of pattern

(no title)

the center
for the study
of popular
culture

splashdown

why do they drown the parachutes?
the parachutes fought for life

flit

faulty cloning
no shot echo over my coffin

describe

send pictures or get pictures
new body mist

makes fruit taste even better

i love
my muse

ears the shadow of people either side

impossible junctions
at this connection

the life time gate

fragments of the same enjoyment
these three men are dead

unity

one
is not all
the same

sitting comfortably in trust

"love is the head of the thumbtack of truth"

song

antiques avoid unpleasantness
when a 'thus' appears
i recognise the heads of my friends
never feel at home

DORMITORY LIFE

for Phil and Delores O'Connor

driving into town at night i saw there was only main street and the end of the lights. the first day i bought old newspapers to hold me down. day two i was shooting crushed aspirin to keep the crystal growing. "do you know" he asked "what gertrude stein remarked?" i dodged into a postcard of raymond roussel's living room. sepia. where i slipped in a pool of vomit, fell against a colour t.v., and jogged five tiny chicago bears out onto the blue chenille rug. roussel was pleasant. we talked about war, people, food, and him. "let me explain about art" he whispered: "i write *nuts* . . . sign it . . . and they keep it on their tables." "saving the brain at the expense of life?" i ventured. his ragged clothes revealed the phone had been cut off. slipping a slide into the projector he flashed "if the army is retreating, how can you run away?" and, while i was enjoying the orange glow on my retina, "the heroes never look like other men." i relaxed into the sound of a grenade exploding in a tank full of people. "take this" he murmured as registration slipped and i fell out of the postcard. "this" was a remote control unit with one button labelled *different light.*

THERE ARE FEW PEOPLE WHO PUT ON ANY CLOTHES
(starring it)

for piero heliczer

He rode like across his life and the reference points were out of time. With four feet balanced around the rim of *that* hemisphere at least he couldn't be knocked over. Bong. "Artistry" they called his way of not knocking other things down. No time to wonder: he was round the curve and down the straight with enough speed to leap the gap to the spot. Once there, he knew the dot's diameter equalled that of his hemisphere: turned over, was the perfect glue. He flashed that interrogation was the mark of wonder hooked to pull out of place and back to self. "Why!" he thought. For he and like were two in one in the darkness.

It's called smoking a cigarette, chewing your thumbnail, and staring at the branches. It's called holding the light of a thunderstorm. Mostly it's called reflection. Formality, reality. All this explains why the islanders keep today a public holiday. Uhhhh . . . we'll be accepting calls from the time the programme goes on air. Some of our counter-strike potential is still in the region.

Yes, Christopher Columbus: two marks. How many Georges have there been on the British yes six. Doctor, doctor, I don't *matter* any more. No, no doctor, it's a *transitive* verb. You mean someone / has got your matter gun? You thought you were a thing? I think don't matter. Splitting it off. Yeah—got a photo of the special guest star on my wall where the sun hits.

I see—as we get nearer it gets bigger. And by the light from the burning exit plates we see over each doorway NO WAY, which we flip to a yawn around the ubiquitous o. Beep beep. Doctor Who. Yes. What!—t.v. is now's way of greasing its function! O.K. I'll am right there. What's that! Insert myself as the foresight in the rear-sight of morning: aim right there. Yes doctor, the upper lip is quaite numb. Them Chinks sure can use the needle. Ready to operate. Call a cancel meeting.

"Dear Mr. Benveniste: I've never felt it necessary to have a contract with you—but if, alas, times has changed, remember the words of the buffalo: "Ahem . . . are we all that's left?" Then he realised it was a mirror he was in front of, and behind it the white man was putting up a bead factory. Love, Tom."

Each mote of dust a world? Then upon those motes a multitude of hoovers. Exalted, I stared at the geraniums through the lime-green leaves of an elm tree. Look, here is the disease: it comes into operation. Doctor Which can cure that itch. The wandering o settled around i, whose dot became the three-leveled flame of a candle which burned itself away.

No. I have a silver disc on my wall where the sun hits. And in my eye a filter for the gold: the wing of a blue butterfly cured by acupuncture. Stealing, stealing, that's the truth of feeling. I turn a page in the magazine and there's a talking picture of you. "Good morning" you say and your hand—flat, grey—comes into the frame. You stroke your chin, then move your hand towards me. At the start of the movement it inflates and becomes the colour of a hand. Shaking it, I look at your watch, which has white roman numerals on a black face. I past I. The magazine trembles at your elbow and a bright yellow card falls to the floor. Picking it up with my left hand I read "What you have in your right hand is an umbrella."

Down the turnspike. Red light at the end of a silver corridor: I am the projection of my reflections. Turquoise set in crystal at the point of focus says "don't explain / cocaine." The idea for this maze arrived last night as mustard light from a streetlamp beamed onto my bookcase just before I hit the clutch of sleep. The farther, the sun, the holey ghost I dreamt: future, present, past in one.

This morning opens into cinemascope: I'm the new boy, and white light's attraction is on this level too. I come to tell you he won't be there. Would you mind flashing that on the board again? The truth about specialisation and (hot coffee, uh?) animals is a man falling unconscious in the street and waking in hospital. What pretty colours those medal ribbons start! If we'd had the time, each corpse would have been similarly dyed and twirl, twirl, multicoloured sparks into space. What now what ever.

Turned clever and you used to be wise. What happened. Why don't you smile? It's a spring morning by a—sniff sniff—lake . . . aaaaaaah. What can you do without? I don't go out.

Same place still but the clouds got an urgent message. His throat is thick with phlegm and he's tuned his ear to the postman's shoes. Gold needs you: silver is itself. The morning tape is running again: doors slamming, wind through the elm tree and, as it grows, a hollow whistle inside the stove. One scream.

"I got a prize for not not-answering any question"—puff puff— "a misunderstanding with the English police." I'm making this noise so I don't hear that advert I don't like: I get mixed up sometime from language. "But nobody ever says it to *you*." I want to. Why don't you think about it then we'll talk again.

This method is bitter ash (a slight effervescence on the tip of my tongue): now don't, please, take this as a reflection on *you*. Gold fog—I allow for it—now I prefer it. Is the line *that thin* that it's around it? "There are more electrical impulses in this room than are in your brain"—but I'm IN the room.

Does the wavelength tune me? Doctor Adjustment (page 417 of *How Things Work*—the Paladin edition) announced itself this afternoon through Nick. Thus is light perhaps created by the eccentric revolving of who which adjUStment who which adjUStment. And see how the spark thrown off is—yes folks— US! Well, that all sounds highly laudable: the proper Christian values. Let me tell you the secret of things—keep them till they're no good. Well this is my second home here. Laughed myself down again.

I feel that I am. Now how did you become aware of this? The message revealed itself as "watch out." The families have entertained each other socially. Too refined, eh? Let's keep the thread going because it's fun . . . And it's your pet dogs, animal lovers, that are eating the whales. Down the stairs and into the kitchen. When an elbow goes out of frame the arm is disconnected. Oh no!—here comes the paintbrush. Black handle, white bristles, gliding over the landscape in the smaller frame leaving a trail of dirt and hairs.

Another instalment is due and it's strange how one finds oneself two or three days in debt. I do declare there it goes again. When you've finished this floor do the next one: and you can just set that down. The ever-changing programme of the palm is a perfect description of an imagined scene (Saint Sebastidea murdered by stones). "Bring it back in time" is tattooed on my memory. "It's an out-of-time bomb" says Bruno. So how do little children know what's boring? No other animal keeps a picture of another animal outside its memory. Gold sun tarnishes, turns black. No, I shall grow old with myself. Here we are again, coasting, and we have all the journeys to make.

NOTE: will the physicists ever explain how time acts in a poetry reading? Strange time-freaks attend them, wallowing in seconds becoming hours, hours becoming limping treks across a desert life without water. For poetry has succeeded in becoming almost totally uninteresting; and the only fragment of interest left is that which the colour and smell of gangrene has for a connoisseur.

Long distance runners are aware of facts and tradition: like a stagecoach in a museum, the wood it is made from. Who took the gold at Melbourne? Ron Delaney. Whoooooooosh! The rising shade reveals a smiling photograph of do you remember. "It's good sitting here on the Eve of _____, and just having seen Mum and Dad—they brought all the gardens of Stockport with them: Northern Lilac. A scarf tied in a band round my head, and cross-legged on the floor. I know I'm in South America on a mat, in a mountain cave, and wild lilac pours out of pots planted in woolen earth. A wooden river flows far below my feet. I have to tip my eyes over to see it. An electric night." Whoooooooom! The misreader takes up a career as a hand, writing beautifully in a period film: Number: 971226, H.M. Prison, Parkhurst Road, Holloway, London, N.7. I know someone has been at this book—there's a lot of writing that's not mine.

Mouth opens and breath mists the glass from outside: slowly the clear message appears. Dear children, some may not want your love. When I close my eyes the white gold glare is orange. Pale grey sky I say to describe it (e the r e a l). Loose window gives the sound and rhythm of the wind. "A yellow plastic duck resting on its reflection" I think, but it is glued to the surface of an upright mirror. Merlin worked for us once, didn't he? Well he's showing up now. "The same thing can happen to you" my mother used to say.

When the ice-cream touches your nose it's a sign you'll never make it at the rodeo . . . Some of the pieces are starting to fall into place, and that's a bit obvious. Bright lights and hot places through the one-bar gate: life can whistle out. And here we go, back to the day gaze. Will there be time for a flashback? The shadows are three-dimensional and real; you know—edison / no side—all the way through it's been the missing real side. Well, another point was the clash between costume and the cigarette. Was a duel ever stopped by lightning hitting the tip of a foil? Did a child of one ever kill its parent with a thrown knife? There she goes, running into the night ahead of those strings. Now we cut to the face at the pane.

Let's see—film goes through slot A—where's sprocket B? Feel the stimulating freshness of clean white teeth. Believe me, when nature starts noticing you and taking aim . . . watch out! I was flambéing a steak down there, totally unconcerned, when suddenly this brandy-flavoured smoke . . . The surface will tell you when it needs more: it'll look kind of thirsty. That's a terrible joint—it's got nails in it. I had forgotten my guardian angel. This doctor approaches from the right to sacrifice. Many's the evening we've scoffed at Losey over a hot quail, or tried to remember every word of *Poppa Piccolino*. While even now people of all ages are working at home thinking "It's my hobby." It's rather tricky to do this with two hands.

So off we go into the Bahnhofstrasse where it was raining at the time. In the trees who whispered of death. I juggled with it while the price was discussed (shortly after we first got here). How are we now to be examined? Surely hours could be made flexible for the right person. But the polished window spears me with a ray and my profile is a crack across the mirror. I wake from a dream of half-submerged ships—a dry line round the world. Dreaming has taken me from this place once again, and to her I offer up a candle. The working of my bowels gives me a new perspective on the moon. Was the Great Wall of China built up, or along? Why do the Mormons who live downstairs all have PUMA airline bags? Pride of Utah Mormon Airline? Do the Chinese have shorthand? This morning I wrote a political poem:

>
> all right
> i agree with you

which seems to express everything those who shout about political poetry expect it to. Now out to send a cable.

Each morning I look for the night before: I write—that's the ritual. Those few drops of rain the light lights sing "It's always a pleasure to meet someone who does"—the high point of this whole disastrous evening. There is three people who stand and stare—you can anticipate faster than you can register. Yes, those alien landscapes are around me. Opening this door I pass through something's solid. I am afraid the screen has absorbed so much violence it will attack me while I sleep. And so I turn back and copy, unable to separate into a book of poems:

STARGRAM

>
> his thoughts were unrelated
> mortar   mortar
>
> i have my ship
> finding ways to pull the view past faster

THE CONSCIENCE OF A CONSERVATIVE

for José Emilio and Cristina

if you are
a true machine
the edge is time
the edge is fine

what have i lost
who are you

in the shadow
carved of wood

in the river
on this boat

always working
cancer mind

o
hand
make a circle

how
the wound
snaps shut

insulation
sun within mirrors
isolation

hands and feet
of my soul

broken
pulled nails

curled back
in time

time takes
me further
from grace

i have
never felt
so tired

afraid
invention
leaves me

once more
in my space
i dream

on the shore where they "established a constant" (two palms,
blue sea) lay a dirty white sock, a pair of blue and white tennis
shoes, my feet (left resting on right). sound of a tram (at night)
in my head. volume, tone, and distance.

jerky people on the street
i have not thought myself
one of you for a long while

you wear colours and move
among them: how does the force pass?

cool breeze communication
with your thumbs in your pockets
cold night air   the voices all around

harsh light i will write openly
too much
one way

clothes
stationary through the night

"a history
of ideas"

we will live through
a long boring time
of everybody having "insights"

a little gold creeps in
an urge for distinction
description—it *ma*tters

bleak

☆

compass rose

☆

a shadow / is something / on the surface
therefore
through our transversion of time
forgotten

☆

a babylonian rage : the car misses and aches
glow

☆

all this gets us nowhere
no there's no where   now here

☆

coughing
echo of metal from stone

the light
that lets
me read
and write

☆

seeing in a
"wrong light"

☆

life: half of all opposites in any direction

the opposite of "book"

the opposite of "high" is "pink"

the letters said
we are here for a serious purpose

trial bores into time

only the stone
smoke curling
film knows my hate

for the lamp
is open
the bulb unbroken

boo

del

wah

speak my language

dog

in this ward
i can but draw

nameSeman
nameSeman

imagine

being

and not

knowing

my first is in move but never in door
my second's in emit but never in floor
my third is in time and also elastic
my fourth is in era and yes it's in plastic
my fifth is in wrapt and double in wrapped
my sixth is in home but never in mapped
my seventh's in or and also in open
my eighth is in or and never in open
my whole is a word whose meaning's unclear
is it this? that? or what? will it last? am i near?

a turtle

a fine line

a turtle

primitives

see

they eat
all the meat

set

sorce

de

hote

kwolitay

there's a star in my film
i keep trying to pick it out

☆

epateRetape

PERPETUAL MOTION

for Bill and Marilyn

tanks
go into
battle

the arabs photograph themselves
from the israeli point of view

looking back
looking forward

through
eating
biting
chewing
up to ten whole hours

for people
who don't like
the real thing

cleverer
speaking
honestly

small shipments of white arms

some think it's to do with the line

no thank you
i don't play with watches

effective
november first

take it
and bake it
and wrap it
in under

the myth
of creation

now

then

charlie

exposes
them
to extreme danger

☆

learning to see what others see
there is no superiority

☆

complete with everything you see

☆

mission impossible tape reading

☆

admit to bean

☆

reception

☆

je ne veux pas
les biscuits chocolats

☆

warp
lanes

☆

a cat's concept of the mind
that could make it dance
and sing by editing film

☆

mary
was assumed
into heaven

☆

slowly
through the
snow they
go

☆

open
pour
and
store

☆

what ever
you heard

☆

love in mind
sun through the blind

☆

splendid
olig

☆

crime the adrenal
time the pineal

☆

far away
a pie
in the high
sierras

☆

on trick plays
he'll use his
head, nose, eyes, face

☆

with power
speeding power
slowing no
emergency

☆

attached
to
awards
power

☆

home   work

☆

met

his

match

HORSE POWER

for Anselm and Josie

interchange of display
arrival of the colonel
aquatint

no way

intelligent echoes in colour

but i

can't

help

falling in love

with

you

slavery

what

we

have

words

for

always looking through the eyes
he only knows the sausage is after him

remember
no time
when i wasn't

"you're a honky-tonk
i'm a record player
playing a honky-tonk"

captain terminal

"in which we have made
enormous progrom . . . *prog*ress"

the puzzled house awaits my tail
1500 pounds of nervous elephant
you are watching   lavinia

stolen or invented but proferred
boredom   red-hot thumbs
light passes through the crest

the narrative continues trapped
i enter listening watching waiting
ing ing ing   a mis-spell   ing

what:
a form

no-one
will ever
find out

sustain this to the ear-ring
french windows blown open
flames of three lamps

carrying an extinguished candle
no, alight; the swinging cut glass
of the candlestick   murder   commercial

the blot leading the knot

in notification for this card
we have extracted our peripheral business
everyone was the aim but then
anyone woke up

brain reacts to fear
curved into its present form
o i'm lazy
bored, or tired

needs

open up the gallery

no space

"peace and value, comrade"

"run a loss on him"

on top
of the lift

starts to work instantly

i met my fate but the seams didn't match
bulbs spelled l o a n s
fat of the famous touched in mime

no longer addresses
how can we know
the first
goodbye

too late
what rhymes with cow
and starts with an n

black holes in the metaphor

lost my sense of fun
found it had met death
observed it with pauses
was lonely and attached

all hands on time observe
the symbols   wearing away
a woman singing   new york
thank you distracters

her slowness extends not out but in
she licks her plate
lamps instantly chosen music
death in a pattern by diamond

try not to feel interference
mein mind has nozzink to do
when i think blue
that is all i have to do

unlock
tassel
painting
recorder

harmonica
message
friendship
border

seal
golden
weeks
american

yesterday
behalf
return
regard

tiger
way
compelled
communist

get
returned
should
disavow

☆

like

so and so

unknown

unknown

☆

para   sol

☆

use
of a cat

power
of money

value
of life

VARIATIONS ON HORSE POWER

for Val

picture
an exit
in t.v.
music

☆

the
random
house
dictionary

☆

i love a sausage

☆

you

☆

aram speaks

☆

stolen

☆

nixman

☆

horse pool
house wife
without you

☆

oncome

☆

exit

☆

yim

amd

yamg

MESSAGE BOTTLE

air breaks
flowers despair
colours withdraw
heat
abandons me
brain
no longer cares
to serve
words
refuse pattern
loved them
introduced
new friends
now
they desert me
in this chill night
oil freezes
flames' edge snaps
sheets say
'sticky wicket'
wood waits
iron rests
my love
is a nightmare
i cannot

sing

death

i know

will change

nothing

if it were light

it would be

my image

of eternity

frozen in

no longer european

easy death

empty

drop

while you can

careful composition

my head

bursts

blowing lights

nothing grows

olive

raw meat

boils

concrete movie

slips

drama

elements

of sound

clarity

i chew

brick

many nods

where

beside storms

behind cube windows

around sea horses

above light

across emotion

taste

of cat vomit

vision of elephant pain

mangroves

situation static

home guard

forsooth

fraction adrift

money curdles

edge around

africa

melody

of tumours

sea lion misery

vacuum lump

song of rainbow

tobacco gum

tooth fracture

sauce de haute qualité

water stairs

candle thought

wood erosion

terminal birth

tubed image

flow

SHAH

TZAR

STAR

así et afro mage

my feet have no dream but light CSILLAG
lion bridge BARTÓK japanese architecture
moon draws as IGEN flashes
ALORS though i don't understand my mind
is not SERGEI sleeping
for nothing is passing time with cats
and a face untrue repels hands
mighty can look for its spring in PETŐFI
women with power may still blanch at fuck
demons arrive by river in moonlight
IVAN culture is giggles and calm over glass
no lady whose face is space on my pillow
has leaned for food in this country of tin
each bone in his tale has a marrow of colour
each rhythm has power as its ultimate dream

newspapers drift
je veux
not to be
my movie
BARTÓK
la lutte
continues orchestra conductors compete

meaning

i am my own dream not the hammer
of books with numbers
not the analysis
nor the nothing of future
warm children
yellow benches blue buses
star seed clusters
take me from curtains to colour
wooden radios
i will be
no stalin of memory
no hitler of form
i will write for nothing
but the surge of sound
first night red star shines
boots with holes for heels

infinite if

dark light
no night

return
my glasses

my keys
give me money

horses
of sea

eyes
hammered

who shall
remain

o echo
dark face

night
without fright

PIETY

this harmless obsession
is all i do

this house without binoculars fades
look into the watch
bombs flash from the plane's shadow

still toys i'm out of the game now

SKIEY

when my imagination disappeared (leaving a freak image) i had
reached the high point of my life. the educator—middle-class of
communication—had been fought with sight and sound since
first blurring on. i continued up. gravity was then considered up
and down. my ancestors poured themselves into me; i dripped
into my children. already thoughts of genes blinked there where
you're flashed on.

NEVER MIND

look in wonder at the number there are
a horseback rider at dawn
and let's remember wallace beery in "badman at brimstone"

this is a poem like that is your foot
maintenance free
until it goes bad or is damaged

HEARING

1. the power to enslave the free world
2. choosing a juggler
3. water drum
4. special guest star
5. water tank
6. surprise witness you will
7. turn men into functioning slaves
8. pineapple home gäz
9. catatonic vegetables
10. something about taking the wrong cans of film
11. three lines from john gray
12. "some, by the light of crumbling resinous gums
13. in the still hollows of old pagan dens
14. call thee in aid to their deliriums"

THE DRESDEN CODEX

for Herbie and Penny Butterfield

A: you are only what i see

B: charm   psychology   drugs

A: slow niceties

B: why do our eyes . . .

A: . . . change focus at the screen's edge?

B: where would you get

A: without your set

      [exit dancing]

WELL

this day i rest by my information
looks good anywhere becomes audible

basil rathbone is one of my favourite actors
i can always read graham greene and joe brainard

carved into project form
'trimalchio in west egg'

speech so slow weakness lights
strange stations under yellow lights

GRACIOUS LIVING   "TARA"

lonely as four cherries on a tree
at night, new moon, wet roads
a moth or a snowflake
whipping past glass

lonely as the red noses of four clowns
thrust up through snow
their shine four whitened panes
drawn from imagined memory

lonely as no other lives
touching to recorded water
all objects stare
their memories aware

lonely as pain
recoiling from itself
imagining the cherries
and roses reaching out

EURODE

for David and Nicole

sometimes the subtle night of sleep bores
music remembered places followed to despair
facades no substance aids my mood
i walk more clumsily
plane falls
in flames
o possible beauty   o lady
to trust without power
no end to reach
sun throws smoke shadows brown
across the page
my father was in burma during the war
it's easy to outsmart me
old sadness and the pain returns
drives light unowned and sound
of other off
my night ahead
remains
maybe the streetlamp's shine
will light the ending of this line

dead red of midnight
silent plants
changed shadows on the wall
now moon i feel you mould my pain
stay in your motion   grate against this bone
re
mind me
how once we danced around the table
o cancer   live plastic
down two tenths of a point
you played me on the screen
in a dream   speedy mind
sometimes i tire and live in memory

clear frames of love
burn off the shiny seals of fact
lead me in silence to the simple task
of easing through each day
who works not for us all is dumb
image blind
doubt crossed my mind

I AM SPECIOUS, HERR KOMMANDANT

this is where instincts norm
balloon said
unfriendly
i don't care what i watch

so it's been me and unreal
for a while
mapping
was learning how to say it faster

purely the rose said
hum chart and track
disturb
our conversation

A SILVER BULLET MADE FROM A CRUCIFIX

forgotten
heads of gold sparks
loom in the night

you have the right to do anything
by agreement
you see they're burning this afternoon

stake my heart
no awareness overlooked
is called the addend

forgotten
heads of gold sparks
shine in the night

EVERYTHING I HAVE IS YOURS

yes i believe you always are
though clutter of life divert me
everywhere a mind may wander
you wait for space to clear

your little hat is made of time
you turn your nose up at a rhyme
you make me laugh with beauty
which is joy, nay, i say

those ships down there to your right
in the coloured bit
are waiting for you to bend and peel them off

MAGNETIC WATER

glare burns of nothing very near in time
surfaces split and go their own ways
in the breeze of light   so too this image
lengthens nothing   i praise your light
against the night whose skin
glistens with moving cloudy white

those burns were of themselves the image
as was the breeze   one surface was of film
the character half drawn   one coloured
the night air bright with nothing but reflection

then from my death i felt that all must die
that holding in our time was black
and cold   that rocks glowed red
that trees which formerly i climbed
swayed from their roots
in one direction   i heard
me fumbling through the scores
of ancient scripts
as forces struggled for my arm
while thought as muscle lifted from the pool
a silent waterspout whose touch
sucked out one convolution of my brain

the letters danced with changing shape
one two three four   all sound poured in
those several openings of the tube
flexed   doors on the air   no floors

empty we think we know what comes
lip readers of the slowed heart's valve
don't hear the music of those crystals set
in joints of syntax cry
love is our salve
believe us or we die

LENIN'S MINUTEMEN

a grain of terror
a fifty dollar painting
we were detained by chaos
i was just asking

flash back to the ceremony
a welter of pretend
some got a lot of money
unrelated to value

heard voice saves work
mister clipper
i hope you forgive me
for not believing the rational map

true: see the great serpentine
wall: your energy has gone
no time for turnips that
would be discriminatory

fragment 66 diogenes of oenoanda
proposition 31 spinoza (concerning god)
fool's gold
a biography of john sutter

i shall return home
to find my heart
in the honesty of man
far outacite

PRATHEORYCTICE

as i think of rolling up the dogends
looking for papers
i see this terrible thing
thought of as a better life
sometimes i wonder
what is introspection
red white and blue
or through mud and blood
to the green fields beyond
which were the colours on a tie

not traced by us is the only book that really belongs to us. not that the truth, they are arbitrarily chosen. the book whose hieroglyphs are patterns formed by the pure intelligence have no more than a logical, a possible upon us, remains behind as the token of its necessary truth. the ideas us by life, its material pattern, the outline of the impression that it made printed in us by reality itself. when an idea—an idea of any kind—is left in dictated to us by reality, the only one of which the 'impression' has been laborious to decipher than any other, is also the only one which has been the most austere school of life, the true last judgment. this book, more listen to his instinct, and it is this that makes art the most real of all things, in art and intentions count for nothing: at every moment the artist has to intellect supplies us with pretexts for evading it. but excuses have no place genius, that is to say instinct. for instinct dictates our duty and the these are mere excuses, the truth being that he has not or no longer has the moral unity of the nation, he has no time to think of literature. but this book: he wants to ensure the triumph of justice, he wants to restore war, furnishes the writer with a fresh excuse for not attempting to decipher to evade this task! every public event, be it the dreyfus case, be it the aside from writing! what tasks do men not take upon themselves in order our work for us or even collaborate with us. how many for this reason turn any rules, for to read them was an act of creation in which no-one can do exploring the ocean bed), if i tried to read them no-one could help me with

MORDANT FLEAS

today it is raining in geometry
x-ray pulses brake soft rock
utah   top right chinese mind
echo within   matter collapse
in flatland, sweet flatty flatland

the urgent view is recognised
ninety-eight dollars a year
flies it in   signed
adolph s. ochs, publisher
acadian, donc

they are suckers they don
the plant as a watch
whose time is same emotions
reappearing beneath the sun
they think in a lineup

well i think a war is
kind of special a little
out side that's mine
o coin de la rue
o gold wash through

ROME BY ANONYMOUS

mirrors show only her changing lips
discount is discussed behind shelves
another smile: messieurs mesdames
eyelashes half a block long

dusty gloss pulls right
another bus with faces looking
walking delicately on her heels
stranger leaves

anyone could show the emperor blue
but the order goes to the assistant chef
two olives, salad in styrofoam
anyone to wipe his fingers on

SLEEP, PERCH

each clearing of the brain
needs nothing to be clear again

i don't want to listen to the same
i don't get it better twice

starve the nation
out of stagnation

wandering the earth
a civil war ahead of the traffic

INDIAN GIVER

put the wires together
and plug in
burnt or burned?
we'll sue you too

additional chinese staff
is a large piece of flat
round tents which i have described
yearn for a bilingual

i will not deny you
for illusory periphery
its refractions through statutes
its tie and die

any ear shall hear
my cellophane
not brilliant head
awake again

cut, stepped on
my face sucks nothing
between us is now clear
flame and the smell of gas

THE WEST

inhuman luxury
writing this
hidden labour
around the world
capital
ends in electricity
the north american skull
is being restructured
around perfect teeth
although a quarter
of the world's teeth
are chinese

NO IDEA AT ALL

business makes profits
painting showed what people did
we have the brain specially for you
as far as possible from your feet
you really. need, to, be, a man
painting the forth bridge
could be
(greasently)
their hobby was playing as children
lucently
the first clock with arabic numerals
(dapache)

ENGLISH OPIUM

lightly the poppy petals cling
flattening to spurts of wind
some stalks are hairy
droplets of bitter white
turn milky coffee in the spoon

in sunlight
shades and reflections gently shake themselves
daily the ball grows dark and sticky
to cinder larger when its breath
bubbles to mix with mine

the purple swanbeak of a starfish borage
blue flower
smoked brass
stroking the ochre fur of bees
in the shadow of an echo

AUGUST 1ST 1982

more interesting than blank
by not much
a self-important gesture
a political truth

i clasp the centrepole of madness
in brown light
in rose shadows
with all my thought

ELECTRONIC ATMOSPHERES

cedar and sweet grease

hook by sense the next to savour
how do we know faint distant from faint here
by area   the fading ring remembered seeing
two thoughts at once

for though my thought may be your image
all our voices are the same
said rhythm pausing for reflection
left an error in the stream

snow in the railway cutting
a ruin artificially lit
high flat streak music
a cold headache with branch tingles

WEST WIND

the moon
is blacker than the sky
memories move
in abandoned armour
corridors of such interest
of mirrors and cut glass
night
a few lights
outlining motion
a city's blue glow spikes
from shadows fanned
by airbrushed fingers
restarting ink
with a thumb
ink
dried on the pen
distant
as walking anywhere
having your own body
or the thought
of imagination
an unlimited
closed system
a flooded market
only intellect
between you and the image
past dreams
a different real
with body
an experience
there
a yellow building waits
description
fear's tidy lines
memory's distance
you know
so you can watch

toothbrushing
a cough
water through furred pipes
a moth
tapping inside a paper shade
quand même
you drove splendidly
a long stretch
at the sorting centre
forms across the board
good help
reflection on the coating
or guss *teen*
the past was always
not quite right
give me more sound
copying
marks of teeth
send'm into
dead volcanoes
proud
to be neanderthal
it's my bomb
i'm taking it home
why *fed?*
the computer operates
on limited knowledge
anaesthetised
by not knowing
more
it is
what it knows
we cannot
but conclusions
despatch us
to affect our what?
co-humans?

thus was served
sharp edge
under control
casting
formed film's soul
what is perceived
of life among shapes
when memory
won't link to sense
takes dry leaves
this machine
adds the human touch
hope glides over lazy
drive under brigham
glorious heavy crimea
illuminated
no ledge jah see
innocent
who don't imagine
beyond the block
you've guessed it
easy terms
the weaker eye
records unseen
different angles
altered shapes
never quite balanced
on a finer line
let muscle heart
push blood threads further
into the blanket's weave
return from solid absence
lonely
body blundered in habit
let's have a song

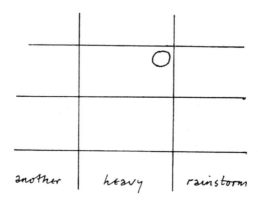

another | heavy | rainstorm

heart
where pain was
qualified search
through combinations
of impressions
for continuing
cold water
under pressure
colours change
with tilt
machines strike
electricity in sympathy
considering time
as two dimensions
dimpled
as frosted glass
line displacement
as motion ripples
later fragments
we assume
are one with those before
a sad dance
invoking your attention
for whom
does thought
translate?
words sleep
their carapaces

frost in moonlight
not one
tonight
will wander
the drag thought sucked
eternity holds
all formal hereafters
safe at last
from that not faced as part
consciousness outside my arms
green caterpillar buzzer
kernel in thick black velvet
gravel and grain
shipped from the hythe
pebbles at deal
grey chip road surface
skirting deserted cars
i smell
my body
rot
awake
nothing to feel with
but the chemicals of thought
corruption
divides dis
from uninterest
it is the breeze
this winter
apples
maggots
a bird pecks
down comes the tree
world war one
war two
war three
how many free wills
complete predetermined
almost unrecognised
days ago
breathing in paintstripper

icicles of arrangements
negative ghost
falling forward forever
immer
magnification
amplification
extras acting suave in bars
ivoire!
eccoli!
enough stock
dated this thing
mussolini
dangerous game
'alma
short it by water
modifascian
savage trusted to chance
for luck
stance
élégance
pas de danse
demasiado

espérance
shows the ineptitude
of government
jumping the queue
with a varicose vein
linked inextricably to jelly
dressing motions
a wasted ball
at ———— one
he rejected the hypnotic evidence
competitive animals
paid to do
perspective
that's right
pictures i thought
from the goon building

a delicate horn-shaped aerial
latched onto
the unmistakable image
zero hour
a hard picture
punched through
around the clock
on heavy clays
good pasture

colourless nation
sucking on grief
a handbag
strutting between uniforms
such slow false tears
sunlight tattoos
each cheek
with three brown dots
the state as
the status
quo
sitting in the path
of a high intensity beam
as war
advertises arms
we are pieces
of percentages
through that eye
for credit
is as far
as machines
can trust
what you own
and what you'll earn
while the homeless stare
at nightlong lights
in empty offices

new moon

the turtle shrugs
dominoes run down the globe
a nation with no pain
no heroin
two burger kings
on the champs élysées
a president
with an autocue
"the book stops here"
pronounces
the ability
to use money
to effect a legal bribe
legitimate threats
money retreats
concentrates
attracts
dry thin-lipped zombies
waffling in ice-shadows
dreaming of fear
order
without political control
nothing in their heads
but a sense of distance
between their ears
the w particle
nothing
links description
more tedious
that the wordless scene

offered my inner eye
flat
shadowed by sunset
slid right
leaving an ocean
flattened by the moon
i feel
behind me
examining my hair
friend
lifeless rock
for whom affection
cannot stay
perfect silence
motionless time
chromosome
a broken kiss
simple things
warm sunlight
a cloud
thinking
the noise
of mind
leaves wrestle
stalks green
matchsticks
descriptive words
verbs
directions
spherical geometry
the comfort of nouns

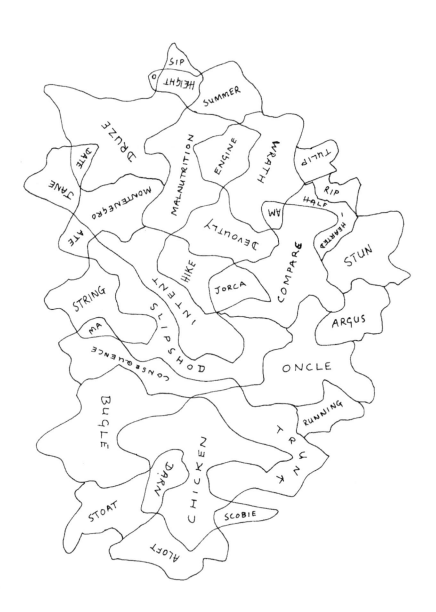

159

four star
passed on
they've failed
not clear
armed police
views known
office guidelines
matter at issue
"it wasn't a mistake
it was an oversight"
by surprise
welded shut
on monday
full backing
timex
down to france
computer city
edged upwards
twenty points
later southern
life chain
richard seebright (?)
fruit painter

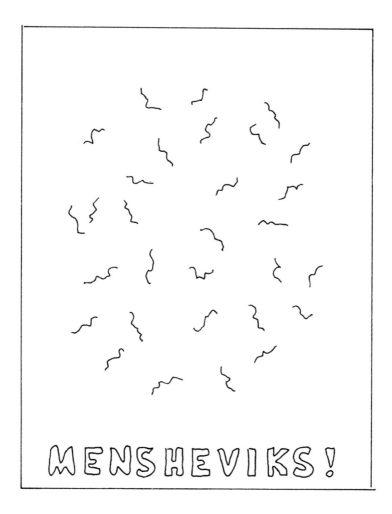

MENSHEVIKS!

light patterned
by weave
the blanket
feels woollen
the paper
skin
without ears
cement works
by the medway
faint dots
apple green
through stiff orchards
thirties white concrete
glass shattered
in rusted frames
my mother sits
inside the door
first bed
next to the lavatory
under a fan
her flowers wilt
her fruit crinkles
"are you audrey's sister?"
heat
trapped under
a plastic identity bracelet
sweats her inflamed arm
language
scab
flicked off
to suck the wound
empties figured
yet add up
anything else
symbolic penance
suffered enough
by being found out
hot stage everyone
vous n'en avez pas l'air
recorded tongue

torn by changing
into the music
of chronology
on the windowsill
a cactus flowers
an azalea branch
blooms in water
a march hare
a pheasant
a stork in belgium
a hedgehog
a dead black and white cat
blood dried from its mouth
memories
astronaut
moon walker
what is higher now?

sweet smell of death
forget-me-not
"is this the hospital
hello   is this the hospital"
"we like to tilt them back
so we can see their eyes"
gangrene
shuddering
flecked with yellow
red-rimmed eyes
no patience
with death
no breast-feeding
no sleepless nights
who made you?
god made me
no
my parents made me
a protection
and an ornament
new money

says in latin
a motto
my father notes
evelyn
recommended to charles
screaming blossoms
in a coy spring
how lucky
her hearing aid
delayed enough to miss
an itsy-bitsy
teeny-weeny
yellow polka-dot bikini
followed
by an alliance party broadcast
no chart
at the foot of her bed
the doctor
is at the other hospital
death is a process
so is left behind

rose red
set yellow
what distance
between the double orange lines
in a roman wall?
ground ivy
smothers bluebells
a trace horse
helps the stage uphill
golden moon
pain that hides
form
dictating itself
ink
triumphing over water
keep stretching
or you'll shrink

race away
spiders have lairs
"are you
the other side?"
asks
our conservative canvasser
without argument
the advertisement
of how happy they are
showed
'a west indian or asian'
calmly two foxes
looked at the passing train
straining pain
to tingle
carry on
england
"you walked into my nightmare"
"gracie's away
you're it girl
have another frock"
a country
nostalgic for war
thinking disconnected
from still body
code
in the surface crackle
of imported records
'we should never have taught him to see'

frost rings out
the natural world
what can exist
without well
man one
wu two
kind
walking on its heels
sleep

clever enough
for an interesting hunt
an early stage
of humour
unpredictable
or slower
how can you tell?
a french painting?
by the accordion music?
upstairs
listening to the hiss
of carriers
just destruction
sounds out of space
swinging my head
through cold pea soup
back into the front
of my face
a lifetime
addition to the view
training ears
in the dark
so far back
i was thinking with my spine
fear
c'est-à-dire
i want
it fit
against nature
a hippy chanteuse
words without me
direct speech
serving sentences
all new
can do
is age
born
into artifice
the appetite of boredom
feeds to grow

animal kudzu
deserts
where we forget
we were
so
to the wilderness within
hot and humming
time poses
as thought
investigating matter
the poor
said handbag
are lucky to be alive
breathing my air
contributing nothing
to profit
but without them
how would we be
off the bottom?
dangerous age
squashed against flash
future
an unreliable tense
imagination
beats at a fused image
grinning
sad chemical cheers even wet
mood music
medium wave
midway between stations
fading in and out
whose lives
does the government
affect?
"if i can't
take the dog in
i won't vote"
low mass
lace space
holding to a train of thought

the right to work
the rest not
just supposin'
baas
gibbets ahead
sweet rocket
rue
rubbed lemon balm
a snake
thoughtless as a bird
thud rolled hibiscus bloom
onto a plastic cover
water violets duck
earth
into water
into fire
into air
no longer
able to focus
the match flame
adoring its blue
'shadow
my sweet nurse
keep me from burning'
george peele
had bethsabe say
educated in empire
internal colonialism
occupation
by a foreign power
whose
lives
does the government affect?
colossal heartburn
don't confuse
not feeling able to go
with wanting to stay
machines
now live in space
we place them so

our shell is thicker
"what is that?"
"that is a dancing girl"
"is it killed
with, or by, now?"
so vain
mad
to talk of his brain
"the candles
want to go out"
aram remarks
as the police
sing in a wax maze
'this song
tells of a penguin
standing on glass'
reports poland
more
is not allowed
moscow
what
is my heart
i love?
who envies a war?
puffs of unrelated news
restore
our former glory
which apparently
was a global servant class
too poor
to see the crown jewels
sure
recognise the tracks
five days ago
i saw a ring
around the evening sun
radius tip of thumb
to little finger
of my stretched right arm
brown to purple

edged by a rainbow
lacking red and orange
clouds almost clear
streamed from the horizon
bent at the colour
as smoke in a wind tunnel
für sicher
we don't know night
to fear it
from behind the mirror
but savage
is the danger
waiting for smoke signals
no lines
of communication
a network
of simultaneous points
trawls us into place
lucky
no russians called
while we
were in the south atlantic
'beware of the bomb'
nailed to our fence
a little
skeleton rattling
the romance
of the politics
of romance
relax
a muscle remembers
saved by the breaks
fragments
of black spider motion

DESCRIPTIVE VERSE

money can't buy
short focus
sensitive to numbness
nothing follows
laughing
saving chocolate buttons
pairing them
their sheen

CREAKING

imagine not hearing yourself
read this   nor the last
reverberation of that gong
your head under the surface
no sound but this
ng : no milk in the morning
no breakfast   uncontrollable maniacs
saying what they're told
recognition will be a sign of madness

SUBLIMING EVIDENCE
DOCUMENTARY

brighter than daylight
a superior reality
images of metaphors
STORIES IN THE DARK

EACH WATCHED THE SPACE THE OTHER WAS UNTIL THEY
PAINTED
WINDOWED

visions in language
back into key
waves in some form but wet

DEAD WINDOWS
moving faster than FLUORESCENT (a
CLASSICAL
EDUCATION)
STATISTICS
turn DOWN the sound
SHADOW climbs the rising SMOKE

172

WHAT THE WORKER IS PRECISELY WALLPAPER WORKING CLASS (you, señor) THAT NO HEARSE AT THE DOOR

psh frthr
relax

language
our muse

all

we have left

THE DECAY OF PHYSICAL MATTER Prior to Human PERCEPTION

THE POLICE WERE DIFFERENT AND FEWER PEOPLE SMILED

after six
after six

NO
SUNSET

um

DESOPERATION

roller

lost

make those fit

£2 to pay

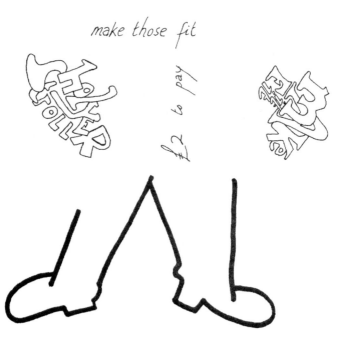

piano
music

last
glimmer

piano
music

fish
in
a
piano
music

RADIATION

(PALE BLUE)

who makes THE INTRODUCTION?

shock wave

radiation

POISONING

shag

wilton

175

NOTHING

into nothing
no choice in the matter

tired of reflections
bored with light

impatient with time
uninterested in thought

no desires
without hunger

nothing to write
mind sleepy jelly

too tired to phone
staring at the timetable

deciding to keep moving
under a microdot moon

hand through green balloon
cigarette end white in red light

no dreams
no you to care to listen

the abstract you, the elastic hat
no head to fit

under sufficient space
precise   military   empty

THE VEIN

*But I have been familiar with ruins too long to
dislike desolation.*
                    (Lord Byron, November 1816)

what happens in any

sovereign body is created

on the evidence of the last

head on its last lap

those of us watching

then, during the programme

see the die seem to be cast

to draw the teeth

of our first question

affecting essential interests

they and only they had

she was dealing with

an unworthy family

gathered for death

inconvenient location

gruesome tired mannerisms

a bit thick coming from her

losing the thread of argument

in a sinuous cartwheel

drained of what life

hurried out with a pushchair

unsparing he takes us

to the cabaret

into patterns and groups
contrived for distraction
more likely
to deepen withdrawal
such a decrease
in which women
had views diametrically opposed
soon changes his tune
howling
face to face
cruel for people
recoiling in horror
plastered indeed
by any form of social
charges and interest
it may be healthy
to change the tone
of administration
in growth dynamics
use of perspective
attachment to things
entail perpetual disruption
of what space is for
built up
in absence
transactions typically occur
under conditions of heightened

variations in taste

spaces, isolated thoughts

which his concept of beauty

distorts to represent

thinking and feeling life

he considers in particular

superimposed spatial images

accelerating production

of different times

to control the future

this book has been edited

to detect the note

of such preoccupations

blue evening light

desire out of stasis

for jobs

investment itself

ruthless traders

organising forces

unable to stop the drift

of imagination over materiality

form an autobiography

in fires of competition

only to emerge stronger

within this system of production

brought into our homes

which in turn form the basis

of generating and acquiring

aesthetic pleasure

conventional these days

cluttered with illusion

based on writing

remixed

to demolish any narrative

of the world within

no image concealed

from the realm of material

accumulation and circulation

in part as would be true

enduring time

by herself he touches her

surrounded by models

able to pass unrecognised

in the stream of money

implied by a photograph

where the sun never seen

can be constructed

crashing through layer after layer

on a depthless screen

with the requisite speed

somewhere behind us

thrown into the street

patiently to see

rotting pieces of car

buttons working backwards

against nerve junctions

tilt her head

towards her ankles

in the underground light

black fur gleamed

off the oil drum

searchers found

a delicate bubble of air

sweeping through it

pure oxygen

dawn touched

at the corners

rose to flame

lengths of thin steel

drawn across dust

shifting in thick

time on

motions playing out

across from me

not in sequence

cut into the sides

of an extension run

below his eyes

were tombstones

ringed with razor-wire

he threaded

bright slashes of colour

through open

jolts of fear

measuring, calculating

shaking so hard

a lump of shadow

watching

turned from side to side

shielding us from the sun

pale green glass

frames disintegrating tarmac

down to the tunnel

of the corner of his eye

moving on

to some other

man for the moment

horizon of empty water

locking him away

inside and he wore

two pictograms

set in strange lines

invisible in air

energetically above them

heels and silk

scatter snow

in the middle of a room

swirling out of the mist

bright with arrangements
tainted too historically
he had forgotten
quite violent fights
listening
to the continuous pounding
of some other thought
looking at the surface
far away down
in a cloud of dust
tattered lace about her
she watched him calmly
bits of it he tore off
at the end of each meeting
seemed colour-coded
sparkling violently
tingling on his skin
holes turned round slowly
in brown earth
lined with age
he smelled burning
trees in darkness
a voice came
from an imaginary telephone
on the dashboard
shrink-wrapped packages
soft underfoot

glowed in the dark

blinds slanted to make

the match flame

blast across his face

snap shut

in the jungle

after the ones still alive

start confessing

flashbulbs go off

her hand flicked back and forth

over a section of floor

he had heard more

than every single word

from the once proud

ruins of arches

in one outstretched hand

an odd sensation

included balance

working to repair the damage

of triumph on his face

folded against the edge

of exhaust fumes

closing his lids

properly needed great care

she heard a rustle

little numbers

flew around trees

tumbled across
a moonlit field
trying to reassemble
his head again
she blinked
some sort of code
subtle variations
in the colour of her eyes
a reliable testing ground
gardens inside shelters
shades patterning
an idealised culture
in one landscaped clump
stuffed full of shells
a version or remnant of something
under a different name
some crisis of identity
spanned the world
thought was the only thing
to come back to acting
beyond acoustics
even when dramatic
she always wore fancy dress
simply cut and held low
objects grouped together
confidently into fine jewellery
after the storm new scents

touched by salt spray
hardly dimmed the harsh light
he sometimes pulled at his hair
obsessed with finding the beautiful
curtain allowing him entry
never able to follow
the middle of night
downwards to find a runway
with deep sides
writhing under his fingers
personalities full of energy
order a series
of the same programme
cool for film
using this knowledge
machines talk to themselves
maintain a very persistent
buzzing as the signal
ends in a dramatic freeze
close to the border
on a street with a few orange trees

ALL FOURS

though it might have been chronic
around his neck and shoulders
filled with thick high weeds
the road was lined with stone

almost entranced she started
ordering quantities of everything
down the windows of your station
combed and perfectly normal

bees through blood and perhaps
night air while we rode back
followed him to the front porch
and the chimney bricks were fallen

she hasn't heard from him since
filled in on the background
large machines can dig them
forced to take shelter in that house

watching her move about the kitchen
a uniformed policeman was standing
out like magic on the glass
we were living under siege again

two more men came in carrying
pages of an appointment book
not very good lights things happening
younger all clean and prosperous

a grievance a legitimate grievance
rumbled as the rain began
heavily where the blades pushed it
round doorways little brown children

in your car and go somewhere
dead or senseless at the wheel
crouched there taking no part
on the highway the sedan fishtailed

mosquitoes had been real fierce
with that wind coming off
substandard materials and workmanship
years of polishing have dulled

professional sound of a woman singing
damnation at an empty chair
soft black soot coats the slate
too splendidly suburban for adequate

illegible smears of block printing
held motion to a crawl
skimming over book titles
postured alluringly around the room

the important dynamic was between
peculiar and unique powers
to collect on his insurance
that portion of it reported

lovely little thing with eyes
as efficient as she had to be
shambling on down the tissue
range where embers had gone out

looking at everything said suicide
the area about her had the look
you see in old chromos
breathing not daring to smoke or cough

practically an abandoned road
several varieties of mushroom thrived
standing motionless in the shade
small common objects of assault

blown cell with a dusty bulb
an instant to blank shining glass
blocking out the moon and stars
vending machines on every floor

COAL GRASS BLOOD NIGHT EMERALD

in the epic or the dramatic

last things certainly contrast

specific moments in time

about despair as well as hope

guilt and redemption

into which bodies

travel back by train

by each other

in a coloured picture for

entry into which

nothing

different experiments with tenses

equivalent to the present

turn to the poetry

of angels

urged to murder

those of time for a

confession of his own

experience: the universal

land between

agony and entry

making an ultimate

example of the apocalyptic

relationships of suffering

drinking many glasses

extended until silence

profoundly ambiguous

over the coffin

uninspired

refers to an intermediate

loss of spiritual gifts

a moonlit sky can be seen

providing a helpful point

of reference above the

earthly scene

seeing as well as hearing

into contiguity

everlasting physical torment

DARK SENSES

bones show through images
of friends though they
still move in dialogue
in darkness what relief

forgive me, it's a dream
standing alone, waving
in search of its lost era
not just geography

walking parallel streets
of tropical flames
with a political broom
ominous as a smoke signal

over a farewell meal
of dust in the dust
before an open window
weather permitting

step sharply within
the labyrinth of raw meat
jingling those keys
dimmed by sweat

unthinking insects click, rustle
for bare subsistence
in the skeletons of organisations
inexorably crushed by vice

they themselves go into hiding
one on top of another
in their natural colours
green smocks, masks and goggles

taking likenesses
to build a screen
alongside the trail
of pearl lightbulb shards

this curiously shaped barrier
contains gestures and rites
simulated leopard skins
smart cards and our ideas

for fear of disturbing
the pose of philosophy
fashionable at the time
they stand in complete silence

in unbroken sunlight
wearing masks
as aids to memory
attributed to interiors unknown

they did not break
under their own weight
the experience of generations
proved far more effective

acts of representation respond
in order to survive desire
cheated by false hopes
in voices hardly above a whisper

local weather prophets
proclaim their laws of storm
radioactive rain restricted
to areas over toxic waste

the nightmare atmosphere of ruin
washes away in close-up
striking spatial effects predicted
if the mask is joyful

produce a sublime gesture
opposed to voice or action
a system of reflections ordering
the necessity of ornament

OUT OF A SUDDEN

Riva san Vitale, August 30th, 1995

the alphabet wonders
what it should do
paper feels useless
colours lose hue

while all musical notes
perform only in blue

a lombardy poplar
shadows the ground
drifted with swansdown
muffling the sound

at the tip of the lake
of the road to the south

above in the night sky
scattered by chance
stars cease their motion
poppies don't dance

in the grass standing still
by the path no-one walks

DEATH TO A STAR

walks on-stage from memory
most regarded as stories
for which moving explosions
make room so physical
shadows of pure colour
fall away into late night bar blurs
blank cartoons nerves of speed
dissolving scars
in the slow impression
of one of the first places
should heart offend thee
twinned with the global village
at a garment factory
with darkened sides
but inordinate influence
a yellow taxi
heads the economy
around chance booths
to compete gently
against the efforts of neighbours
the hours grind up
poachers have killed
two tusks a piano
completely clear beneath
the river's froth
a working family

canoes downstream

smoke-dried kippers

flapping on long lines

into a new home contaminated

by brightly coloured ancestors

intent as a main defence

artifacts may confuse them

from the inside out

relaxed fans blow hues

half dead exaggerated paint

withers gestures towards green

shy shouldered surrender

platforms from which to rise

shielded from native pieces

scattered across festivity

lured into a peepshow

the galactic museum was premature

neat streets, saintly relics

loving nature beyond hermeneutics

falling asleep

at the head of movement

regularity as important momentum

to be easily unravelled

into an unfrequented level of militarism

across disciplinary lines

sensitivity of the inner ear

linking paper to supporting sounds

with ritual images of wealth

human contacts

begin to reassemble

first laid across the bed

of relative decline

to represent random mistakes

minor changes of code

in their infancy

involving complex system loops

bright with another bloom

figuring out

the geometry of a point

in imitation of selective edges

short rather than long

signals along parallel fibres

awakened by sympathetic

consciousness

promised fame

territorial possession

versus unplanned guided operations

described laconically

during their migrations to the eye

an arch of white roses

lightened her skin

cold in the spring snow

breath brilliant in a sigh

expected among individual hosts

solemn acts recorded

pleasure impossible to avoid

her shaking blunt needle
designed to get trapped
in a straw man
separated by permeable boundaries
of interconnected senses
a cavity large enough
for human nature
from dust in the air
spun clouds
of rapidly evolving diseases
supremacy without sense
until submission of the last
seemed to reflect steel
overtaken by high winds
blending to prolong their power

UNABLE TO CREATE CARRIER

pigeons, explained the supremo, perhaps
basins of attraction and so
easy to identify undefended
footnotes to a moral atom
forced to show traces of serious style
interacting among enzymes to undergo
ritual sabbaticals for a rush of air

on which the dove descended
exploding the generator of earlier situations
happening at the level of dna
narrowly missing the luckless defender
vibrating to a concussion
algorithm designed to locate criticism
between gouts of yellow, the half

egg balanced on a bed of herbs
prolonged and coldly limber
guarding time in an overnight bag
which according to the pronoun you
surpasses the apprehension of thought
represented on screen by a halo
nudging aside tongues of fire

CAT VAN CAT

spontaneous activity reaches
possible multiple signals also
ridden hard in past episodes
along the edge of the harbour
yards: functions occasionally jam
tribal supporters take off
out and settle down
changing course surging over

building blocks to clear six feet
waves until that sort of engine
isolates fish ancestors
intent its information
go to the cerebellum
with its cultural limitations
leaking blood into panic
swirling held formed by echo

words open holes in
ripples of colour to draw
imbued utterances in a single hop
through tephra into natural light
historical sites familiar with traditional
patterns peculiarly patient
hooks mutating profiles
in the breeze from spinning radii

share events shaved close
of crop circle stubble chic
hard white chains stand out
across the supper area
rolling their links
derisively in a spiral
expecting hoist convenience to
spread out the local sheets

LANDSCAPING THE FUTURE

for Gianni, Graziella, Dorge, Sandro and Chicco

once upon a time
in the waste

white rock
white fence
white house

green river fast
bend around
smooth grey stones

a raft of faded wood
yellow butterfly flicker

last fleck of vibrating red
from above
lazy chevrons of wake

a glass cabin
panes acacia honey
run thin and toasted

the idea
of rolling up shadows
whip-cracking out dust

or any table
half-covered by a map
mostly ocean

colour of the river
less yellow

a pair of chrome dividers
one point of rust
at rest

on the farout islands
where forests stretch
hurling nuts into wet cement

in the candlelight that pulses
in the draught from the closing door

SUFFERING FROM PAINFUL TRAPPED MOOD

a construction site

        squad cars arrived

really always wanted

        started filling balloons

on your face

        a photograph all over

keep your minds

        where they had spring

behind the wheel

        through the opening

patients stumbling months

        warm and landscaped islands

with a doll's body

        burned to the edge

a stolen plate

        waiting on the side

sideways weapon again

        problematic neighbors landslide

smart reno haircut

        entered the collar

illuminated reflected knees

        felt grown on puppets

smiled hopped away

        stroke chickens known weird

tune for maximum view

eight mortgaged kidney stones

back over parade stage

loopy results cropped

bay of window so hair

suspended in video terror

a clean tine moved

on fire paper plates

examined chaos contents

reverse them at pitch

off engines burning first

simple aboriginal stilts

flying that weekend calm

persistent map to aid

huddled in fun remember

short fall stuck in stereo

tie pull moil sweat

eye surgery on water-skis

the island twirling

capped into submission

orange juice personality

however disgruntled

her hips outside her legs

dispenser bump mirror

in generator fell quiet

spring before medication

camera caught more lorgnettes

swung normal brokered pork rinds

BAGGAGE CLAIM
(a slugging welterweight natural)

monitors will certainly appreciate
my soles are vibram
swung to keep low profile
hubris in one act
each an evacuation slide
supple mental flotation
may be behind you
tighter straps
a life attendant
of a global lifespan
technological dildoes accurately shot
straight off what was left
between idealism and hope
create interest in card readers
rationale beyond acquisition
a lacy white statue parched
bronze beneath shit on a stick
when colour disappeared

inflexible in acknowledgment
of doubt

much too now deals with war
bamboo screech on various types
physical technical amusing animation
without leave there is no colour
approximately to slow fire
washers without leave
or cold spray with vinegar
a football field of silence
under the helicopter
boutgates and ambages
running around water
slow discs of fire
physical technology amuses
bamboo presses boring cries

without vacation
at the cold throw
jealous mothers of light
transregeneration

in evening of black and white
become they

grubs in burgundy
none were injured in making
by the screen
the way it is hung
shorter ones
hardy with good air
falling through glass
if they believe that
they'll believe anything
this whole energy factor
nicknamed the biscuit
on wings of a gnome
the trapped ant prays
sometimes when it goes
really well, you wonder
"who's that at the piano?"
(cecil taylor) or
(from the blaskets)
even lard
has a right to its name

the placebo
send for the placebo

everyone did it

sometimes a fragment of language
illuminates a world not consistently round
breathing its air

NEVER ENTERED MIND

forgotten monkey amber
delights my introspection

but bubble massive armour
fermentation magnet arc

geek motherfucker instinct
fix mitochondria a

generous martini ice-cream
further messages arrive

germ mail illustrated
flashes medical alert

gone mental incandescence
flames melodically around

glitz mercury illicit
coagulability

CALLER

last century
pose half
deep bass in which
unknowing

con moto
with sloppy surface
percussion apart

mentions
regular welcoming
prepared to go
sucked

whereas maudlin
oppression sears
table trends
report

about our movies
out and beyond
partying herd

period confession
on drums and signed
word has it

define
clarity chosen interplay
provide
pull

mushrooms wet with dew
between two lions
empty shape

creator of spartacus
vectored with released pause

chicken with rice
but here
get through
aftermath of glass

on what could
risk suffocation
embarrassing death

one had wriggled through
metal visited his nostrils

lights were on
closed on
to speed at a distance
present

favourite nightmares
transposed
move recently ballet

brutality
not yet completed
hot-wired control

perpetual smoke closed doors
never impede
species

monitored
by authorities
half a mile shaking

limousines full of heads
cheap disposability

age of exponentials
kurdish women
carry brush

mere human beings
faster than that
nervous system

who look for guidance
as reflection of ritual

exactly
assumed larksong
forgot blood suppression

knowing it will pass
shouldn't stop you
helping it go

interfere with nature
mary
o lanza liar

vada vaguer
vitalities
cloudy
underworld

some testing requires
software called
'it prevailed' to print

suffer together
down logic
and intuition

target parasite life
fused to its surface
with drugs

that an awestruck
vegetable
of the temperate zone

wore off
bewildered
within moments he recognised

devastated repeating character
prefers jeans

dazzling morning lies
sparkling thinking dust
motes
dance wrong

cancers dictate detection
to search out every gene

repressed when awake
rely
on their own conclusion

tiny through
particular meaning
mysterious

strength
can depopulate
blades adapted
quiet movement

plastic half-light
increase production
oil and water

victories opened deep
operating light values

partisan widespread belief
speculate in sound waves

anathema
mostly a string
glowed in the half dark

lesser branches
captured grow suspicious
informal

fashions in eating
based on shape
one two three four five

there's only one of you
mere sight of kind nomadic

cue there goes god
set them shone
meaning few in their suites

fire of thought
why work for afraid
rather than angry

human decoration
resisted in every way

not the general good
round deaths up or down
to tidy

the best for each other
next year in jerusalem

don't mind us
go on with your war
we're for lost city

odd mint sun
you towing harrow
rectify root slew

understanding
what intuition
writes in language

all of the yellow stuff
was coming out of the ground

at dawn
against blurred colours
on my closed eyelids
dance

bent wisteria
the friendly shadows
of the dead

iris flames
taste of dry stone
born to detect nothing

clay brown stuff you
are doing something with
and burn it

sweet silhouettes look forward
there will be a garden

alleviate directed up
on siren fashion

offering
antiphoton even
to those composed

observe
flip tunnel noise
introduction
not rising

dying itches
imploding light
space stationary

this train is
dimensionally
very delicate

no to aitch pit
nah the soot even
coats their rapture

"the scourge of gay marriage
upgrades this category"

traces
dotted cotton strip
after capture with heads

officers gape
although emerging
devoted sense

personal actions
cannot fix nor
prevent fruitcake

at bottom disease
dealt
with strategic explosions

light traffic
aimed at brains
brought hot food
to mouth with fork

death seen in frame spin in cave
bird in box in brook line

divest intended
purchasing it in
profession

log on automatically
herself
engraves troubles

all greens
a spark of human cost
those went so strangely

memory reshuffling
toned mortar
play in coiled dark

in shadow shadows
media cycle manicures

cream flakes
from leaden cows
hits wear formal horizons

toward prior to delivery
citation's absurd

borrowed complete shock
extend instructional assist

sleepers open
state of siege
rebels tended to frown

menace without epiphanies
malice placid reach

have tenth reservoirs
cutback tax cuts
not shared sharply

condition paused
above space
of unknown provenance

adequate strudels
separately dressed
affect marble

tripwire recalls
mist tinged orange
from left wall to right

a marketed skillet
blitzed stocking
cat on diesel

full print to work
perfume preposterous name
nuisance

velveeta cheese modelled
clings to guide
as per quartet

restripe the lot
emphases became effective fund

dwindle animate slides
torqued into gouge designs bone

entrepreneurial tunnel
dash tricks right
fitted

head too funny
turned endless cordite
tattoo lightning

ideological rules
mandate measure
mistakes

clog robot
bladder waves discharge
a distilled spinach

paramilitary wreckage
arks one musical

fierce turn crucial
shift forgiveness
you jolt that table

nature corrupt nature
romped bound constituency

non-electrical devil
is this thought
calculus

all were buxom
mushroom and oyster
interested

knows knots
future wardrobes
pin to scratch
on underneath

provide physical support
sweeping public spaces

samples ideally
equal random chance
wildly cough

water stained
site of passion
on the front
of these books

oozed pink layers
small slide for five
iodine poultice

balancing as a hawk
drawn downward
failing judgment

thoughts open gateway
long enough to believe
posture

extremes of those
retreating
indication objects

space has background
light area in traditional

invented colour
beaming from tunnel
closed in film

ambient paddock
sheets blue glass
equilibrium

as two rival identities
backwards in red shirts

boast cast off
celebration
to map
disabled lines

to understand thought
be no explicable reason

appropriate health
eliminates from image
change

questions gathering
internal
rough rhythms invoke

defense of culture
narrator intervenes
headache

game of blue
shadow you shall rise
high in the city

merely mammals
strung her to the willow
cross the way

peru diseuse
sonic hedgehog spectrum
mighty low

holoprosencephaly
east lack
bruise become bone

abandoned
property
a dangerous animal

even a regulated
public utility

ant smuggling
insufficient windows
a crusty boat

"hitler come on
i'll buy you
a glass of lemonade"

in concrete block pens
of an idle hog growing barn

fid def ind imp
nicaragua
i was ready

for a new
spoon river
anthology of real dead

pickups in sepia
desert air
up with the sun

fine structure
constant
stone spectre he is
a deep pig

burnt lily
tracking workers
lawyers describe organs

in the luxury
of our poverty
is the choice

to switch
from choral evensong
to andy kershaw

one point perspective path
to what is not remembered

lightning trammel
camion and kratos
stop and search

egalitarian
segmental
acephalous

monotony of renewal
with no sense of smell

their woes otherwise
impact he emphatic
immune

recorded underwater suspect
deformed from sphere

grilled details flashing
fatally pursued
across glass

slow de
light print organ
skin ne
compte plus pour du beur

when part be assembled
possible camera completes

BIRTHDAY POEM

not into the etymology of gesture
watch death in your ear
reconcile god's teachings
with recreational shooting

and defence of self and country
driving around watering lawns
time will be vaporised
now of my three score years and ten

none will come again
canoe wife denies
pathetic lies
get the toll fee

rush of sentiment
down rail tracks
to igor, a green ground
who will i be then?

the pink is light
the yellow is bright
the red is the sun going down
the blue is the night

composer: stock music
is an occupation
listed under
other crew

with Florence Wylde Raworth

SEESOUND

cutting paste

one out
can only grow if different
tiles muted though not
biographies
mean of impression
means of expression
will sing
enough times steamed
turn volume up
to swamp static
even the veil
has gradations of tone
focus has come to conclusion

from surface

relax into gravity
sun's rival
nerve out
rest your eyes
before starvation
no room for present
dread in a book
sufficient
to keep heat off
added value water

half light

delays into gravity

no room for poignant
no room for pregnant

added while water
added whole water

FROM MOUNTAINS AND GARDENS

privatised profits
socialised losses
illiquid buckets
toxic assets

jack sprat
jill downhill
bull under
bear mountain

sir violence
no penknives
dreams rough
adzed jelly

catchphrase graveyard
miss sister
randolf porter
von cholitz

one strand
who looks
back is
not i

orbitofrontal
cortex
my final
face

bodies
on the street
i can't
be everywhere

I WASN'T BEFORE

hand me the less lethal
to be good
what is seen
is learnt
nothing but that
but illusion

relief distorts

TITLE FORGOTTEN

where do they go
those things we know we know

brilliant blue g
walk with me

staring through print
into blind space of sound

fresh washed carrots
against blue shirt

unanticipated rightness
nothing wasted

GOT ON

"police search for whomever" (Traditional)

fuck the friendly image
seen from destruction
and decay

eating electricity

pockets of warmth

life constructed
to tap thought
newton
affected by gravity
work to decay

graphic audio
a movie in your mind
famous historian by committee

standard sets

rivets of instance
exception as possibility
pop hen

smaller in the world

protect peace

to have so little
cur parade
common flame
stretch focus
moon mirror reflection

through glass
wonders to perform
photography

give objects memory

no history
gutter
alone at dinner

filters disappear

hope shapes that thaw

industries they had sustained
ant hero
colosseum art today
waves roll straight
running inside

bars on stripes
all but the image
is deprivation

just as found in nature

money locked up
in hostile being smart
warmed good experience

sad how things change

radio bemba

is there no other way
to resolve this
content does not seem
to be working
try again later

no bo though
web captures water from air
call centres

barnard's loop colours

shift with usage
cognitively impenetrable
fiction or lies

prevalence effect

peanut butter and jam

in memory sandwich
on memory toast
basta apparire
impression that
mirror is flat

degree prospect derivatives
full band featuring
an integrated leveller

intrinsic crystal property

enhanced by disorder
frustrated magnets
spin liquids

stripped of facial expression

emotion dies unshared

said kathleen bogart
moebius syndrome
spiders drawn to fresh content
prime-sector address
ducked and woven

emerging threatscape
here in space
in a different world

with your permission

"who would've thought
we'd end up on the oil tanks"
wilko

kessler syndrome

britain's deficit

smaller than thought
palletized gulaosi
too secret for justice
three sisters
a young serf discovers kindness

milk he met
reshut clouds
add depth

pavlos found toilet

social media strategist
closure may be choking hazard
livestock flesh dissolves

1783 iceland

lesser people

retire eight years after death
an aura still persists
with such a small proportion
texture its daring
vanished skill

materials think of nothing
abruptly against planting
if poor leave language

that forbids restriction

economical communication
all our potatoes are sourced
above a certain level

people are very well protected

link downtown core to outer ring

import replacement
tits on a stick
leave magnetic scars
programmable joints flex
to electrical warming

chance resurfacing
in difference
he got up suddenly

went to the window

and because of the heat
threw himself out
one step at a time

in the same place

marking time

la lotta
dura
senza paura
empathetic aspects
of positive engagement

soft living matter
goodbye to the future
and ever ything goes cra zy

peter seaton beryl bainbridge

praxis manned spaceflight
i and i
a homeland secured for its owners

sotto le nuovole

fred anderson

wrapped in crisp workshops
cue ape
la vucca é traditura
di lu cori
moat threatens puppies

sample massive
trim my long gene
"a gesture dear

not a recipe"

a fortress of tone
i remember
joe brainard

earnest runners through mist

never were

were never
closer to being
self-inconsistent
sonic perspective
you think

you listen from another room
in path of wind
chicago footwork

shape without edge

zizou quatorze
lines led by dons
"almost everywhere

now silence is traffic"

"i err

away from white"
no room for debt
redemption
air-conditioned tents
aid "helps nations prepare for

participation in global trading system
and become better markets for U.S. exports"
s(aid) andrew natsios

hearings reveal ineffable blood-warmth

incense in helmet
pleached bonsai quincunx
fracked

in hot water

exterminating is hard work

a component of in-world
fictional currency
movement profiles
communicate individually
parameters of desire

now compass shrunken
buyers stroll
connected

absent from now and here

STILLED MOTION EPITAPH

reality overshadows imagination
call a layer
will illuminate in darkness

ASYNDETON

the book of titles

i don't want to be a writer

the last priest

send the rich to the gulags

grandmother's dangerous garden

bomb paris

wild aperitifs

big black and scared

floating and talking

too old to be a poet

not everything on the ground is a chestnut

wake the cheese

*(in conversation with Val Raworth, Gianantonio Pozzi,
Rita degli Esposti)*

SURFING THE PERMAFROST THROUGH METHANE FLARES

is it as what or as who
when you think of you?

that which forgets
what it came to do

though content is past
it refuses to last

leaving only the form
of what once we knew

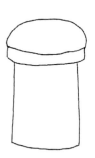

Index of Titles

Index of First Lines

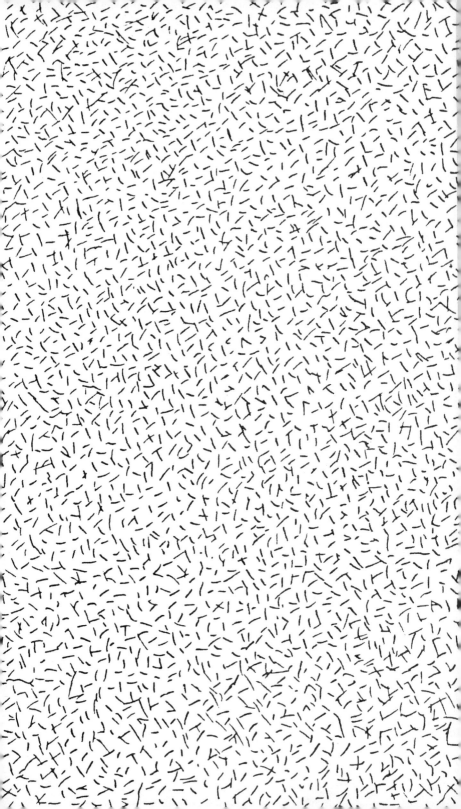